JOHN A...

100
GREATEST
IDEAS
FOR BRILLIANT
COMMUNICATION

This edition first published 2011
© 2011 John Adair

Registered office
Capstone Publishing Ltd. (A Wiley Company), The Atrium, Southern Gate, Chichester, West Sussex, PO19 8SQ, United Kingdom

For details of our global editorial offices, for customer services and for information about how to apply for permission to reuse the copyright material in this book please see our website at www.wiley.com.

Library of Congress Cataloguing-in-Publication Data

9780857081773 (paperback), 9780857082176 (epdf),
9780857082244 (epub), 9780857082251 (emobi)

A catalogue record for this book is available from the British Library.

Set in 10/13 pt Calibri by Toppan Best-set Premedia Limited

Printed in Printed in the United Kingdom by TJ International Ltd., Padstow

Contents

Preface

Communication skills are essential in leading, managing and working with others. The aim of this book is to help you to improve your competencies and capability in the art of practical communication.

Great leaders and great managers are all effective communicators, both one on one and in larger groups, using the written or spoken word as appropriate. Unless you can get your message across and take on board what others are trying to tell you, then you simply will not be effective as a leader or manager.

To be a good communicator, you need to develop your personal communication skills, your ability to lead communication groups and your effectiveness in the downwards, upwards and sideways flows of information and ideas in organizations.

You need to develop your understanding of the nature of communication and the four skills of speaking, listening, writing and reading, particularly as they are used in presentations, meetings, interviews and all forms of communicating in organizations.

The book is divided into Parts and then into Ideas. Each Idea stands alone, carrying its unique message. It is up to you to choose where you begin and end. Read according to your own learning needs and interests.

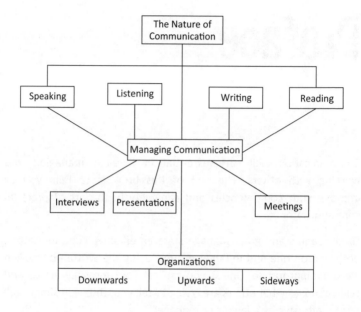

And don't be afraid to write on the book – it won't mind! Underline or mark any passages that are important to you personally in terms of your own *awareness*, *understanding* and *skill*.

This book will give you guidance not only on when to communicate and why it should be done, but also how it should be done. It is concerned with skills in a wide sense, namely the methods you must practise in order to achieve your desired aim of becoming a better communicator.

More than that, I hope that one or two Ideas in this book inspire you to become passionate about communication. After all, communication – in the form of love – is what makes our world go round.

The set of questions at the end of each Part are designed to help you to apply in practise what you have learned – or relearned – in reading and reflecting on the Ideas. The test of the book is the extent to which it leads you to become a more effective communicator. Will others notice a difference?

I do hope you enjoy reading the book and find it useful and profitable. I have certainly enjoyed writing it.

John Adair

PART ONE

Practical Communication

No man is an island, entire of itself, every man is a piece of the continent, a part of the main.

John Donne, English poet

Communication is so fundamental to our personal and social being that it is tempting to believe that it always just happens. But, as you may know from experience, there are situations where communication breaks down or where it is conspicuously absent. Relationships are then damaged and effective work becomes virtually impossible. That is why you need to become a skilled and committed communicator.

Part One is a sketch in outline of the world's body of knowledge about communication. By the end of it you should have a clear view of what communication is, and know the essential ingredients of an excellent communicator.

The Zulus have a proverb: 'I cannot hear what you say because of the thunder of what you are.' What you are is as important in communication as what you say or do. It is always *you* who communicates. That's what makes it such a challenging subject. Are you ready for it?

Fourteen Greatest Ideas for Understanding Communication

Idea 1: Four basic elements of communication

Communication is the art of being understood.

Peter Ustinov

Communication is so integral to being a person that perhaps the worst of all human afflictions is not being able to communicate with others. Moreover, everything we can achieve together in the form of great work depends on our ability to communicate well with each other.

To *communicate* is a Latin word by origin. It means to share or to make common. As the English language developed and became more specialized, communication came to mean specifically the act of sharing in the *mental or non-material realm* – such as ideas or feelings – especially, but not exclusively, in and through the use of words.

Communicating usually implies both intention and means. In a sharper focus we could say that communication is essentially the ability of one person to make contact with another and to make himself or herself understood. Or, if you prefer a slightly more formal version, *communication is the process by which meanings are exchanged between people through the use of a common set of symbols.*

Intention and a common set of symbols – usually combined to form a language – are immensely important factors, but they should not be allowed to fill the whole picture. Emotions or feelings, for example, are non-material. They are certainly communicated, sometimes intentionally but more often quite unselfconsciously.

Nor is a common set of symbols involved. Emotions often do not need words. You should always bear in mind this much broader backcloth of communication, which encompasses such phenomena as the unintentional and direct or intuitive transfer of states of mind or feelings.

You can see that there are four elements implicit within communication. Of course, the whole process will always be more than the sum of these four parts, but each of them is an important factor in the overall story.

Key element	Notes
Social contact	The people who are communicating have to be in touch with each other
Common medium	Both parties must share a common language or means of communication
Transmission	The message has to be imparted clearly
Understanding	The message has to be received, properly understood and interpreted

> **Remind yourself**
> The concept of communication embraces a wide range of meanings that circle around the idea of *sharing*. That sharing or exchange is now more commonly related to abstract things, notably meaning.
>
> For communication to happen there are some necessary elements or conditions: social contact, a common medium, transmission and understanding.

Idea 2: Why is there so much misunderstanding?

The peoples of the world are islands shouting at each other across a sea of misunderstanding.

George Eliot, English author

Why is there so much misunderstanding within the human family?

One obvious cause is the lack of a common language. But, as those who speak the same language are all too often aware, virtually anything that we say to one another is capable of being misinterpreted and misunderstood.

Not only is our speech an infinitely varied weaving and interweaving of 40 different sounds, but the resulting words are capable of many different interpretations. Hence a man or woman can convey or communicate much more widely and more deeply than a chimpanzee can with his fellows, but at the risk of being more misunderstood and more isolated than any in the animal kingdom.

That is our human predicament. If I may repeat the point for emphasis: with our infinitely richer potential, we are capable of attaining a communion with our fellows that is beyond the reach of even the most developed animal, yet our communication is much more likely to go wrong. We are far more prone to being misunderstood.

 Ask yourself
Can I think of two recent examples – one at work and one in my personal life – where I seemed to be talking at cross-purposes with other people?

Idea 3: Communication is two way

Conversation in the United States is a competitive exercise in which the first person to draw a breath is declared the listener.

Nathan Miller, US author

We all know conversations like this: two people talking not *with* each other but *at* each other. Two monologues, with pauses for breath! Remember Adam and Eve?

Thus they in mutual accusation spent
The fruitless hours, neither self-condemning

The English poet John Milton's evocation of the state of Adam and Eve's relationship, after they were expelled from the Garden of Eden, neatly captures the barrenness of one-way communication with neither party really listening.

Real communication is very different. It is as if two people are working together in order to clarify, discern or discover common truth of some kind or other. This communication has a three-part structure:

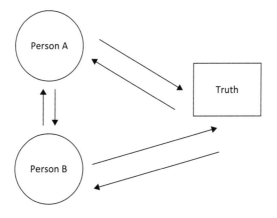

That third element, which I have labelled truth, can have a thousand forms. When you are talking to your doctor, it may be about what is wrong with your digestive system and what is the best method of treatment. If you are the first violin player in an orchestra, the truth you are trying to elucidate with the conductor is how best to play Mozart's violin concerto.

Notice that in both cases – indeed, in virtually all cases – the communication really has to be two way. The patient has knowledge of his or her symptoms that the doctor needs to hear. The leader of the violins also knows the concerto well and can contribute to the truth of how it should be played, with this orchestra and on this occasion.

It follows that if you really want to be a great communicator, you need to be a great listener as well as a great speaker. And you need to keep your eye on the ball, which is that common ground of truth, whatever form it takes, that the communication is about. 'It takes two to tango', as the saying goes. It certainly takes two to communicate.

> *'Communication is dialogue.'*

Idea 4: The model of conversation

No, Sir; we had talk *enough, but no* conversation; *there was nothing discussed.*

Samuel Johnson, compiler of the
first English dictionary

Dr Johnson distinguishes mere talk – the exchange of human sounds, as if to reassure ourselves and others that we are human beings – from real conversation, which is always *about* something.

As Ordway Tead puts it, 'Conversation is the fine art of mutual consideration and communication about matters of common interest that basically have some human importance.'

Real conversation is:

◆ Face to face
◆ A two-way process
◆ Informal
◆ Sincere and open
◆ Adapted to the situation in which it occurs
◆ A means to an end
◆ Desired and enjoyable

Communication tends to be most effective in direct, face-to-face situations and to become less effective the further it gets from this ideal. If one person cannot see the other person, for example, something is already lost from the equation.

The most effective communication is like a purposeful conversation. And what is more, talking to each other in this personal way is also one of the most enjoyable pleasures life affords. As Scottish author Robert Louis Stevenson once said:

Talk is by far the most accessible of pleasures. It costs nothing in money, it is all profit, it completes our education, founds and fosters our friendships, and can be enjoyed at any age and in almost any state of health.

Idea 5: Reciprocity

We cannot live only for ourselves. A thousand fibres connect us with our fellow men; and among these fibres, as sympathetic threads, our actions act as causes and they come back to us as effects.

Herman Melville, author of *Moby-Dick*

The reason that communication is essentially dialogue and not monologue lies very deep within human nature.

In fact, *we become persons only in relation to one another* – and that entails mutual giving, receiving and sharing. The Bantu-speaking tribes of southern Africa have a word for it: *ubuntu*. The concept this indicates means literally 'I am a person because of other persons'. Hence the African proverb: 'It takes the whole village to raise a child.'

Reciprocity is at the heart of being human. Reciprocity means the return in due measure by each of two sides of whatever is offered, given or manifested by the other. Usually, therefore, it implies not only a *quid pro quo* – a 'this for that' – but an equivalence in value, though not necessarily in kind, on each side (as of love, hate, understanding, courtesies, concessions or duties).

You might think, for example, that the communication between a human mother and her baby is entirely one way: all giving on one side and all receiving on the other. But that is not actually the case.

Research shows that human mothers instinctively *teach* their babies in the first year of their lives to be reciprocal. From about six months onwards, mothers naturally start giving their babies objects and encourage them to give them back. By twelve months there is an equivalence of giving and receiving such objects between mother and child, accompanied of course by smiles and warm sounds.

In other words, what mothers do quite unconsciously is to establish the foundation of reciprocity, the basic building blocks that we need to become human beings and individuals. Gorilla and chimpanzee mothers, by contrast, don't do this. They don't need to, because gorillas and chimpanzees are not destined to be persons.

> **Remind yourself**
> Reciprocity is essentially a moral concept: what is exchanged between persons may be different in kind but it ought to be equal in value. We call it fairness.

Idea 6: Nine forms of body language

Nothing is more confusing than the person who gives good advice but sets a bad example.

Anonymous

Caressing, embracing and holding hands are as much ways of communicating as is human speech. Body language, as it is now familiarly called, is something we use and observe throughout our waking hours. Everyone, for example, can interpret a smile or a threatening gesture. And the voice conveys more through its tone or volume than simply the words spoken.

Although we have evolved language as our principal medium for communicating with each other, we retain non-verbal communication, just as a sailing yacht might have an auxiliary motor. *It is especially important as an expression of relationship.* In Japan as in African tribal society, for instance, how near or far you sit from the door indicates your seniority.

When humans come to an exchange of emotional feelings, most people fall back on the old chimpanzee-type of gestural communication – the cheering pat, the embrace of exuberance, the clasp of hands. And when on these occasions, we use words too, we often use them in rather the same way as a chimpanzee utters his calls – on an emotional level.

Jane Goodall, *In the Shadow of Man (1971)*

We can distinguish at least nine main forms in this 'undercover language' of non-verbal communication. They are:

Facial expression	Body/posture
Eye contact	Proximity
Tone of voice	Physical gestures: hand and foot movements
Physical touch	Head position
Appearance (clothes, hair)	

Take eye contact as an example. Video recording of conversations shows that the talker tends to look away while actually speaking but glances up at the end of sentences for some reaction from the listener. This usually takes the form of a nod or murmur of assent. The talker gives the listener a longer gaze when the talk has finished.

There simply isn't space in this book to cover each of these forms of non-verbal communication in detail. But what is important to understand is that the basic system for communication is the human body, not only the organs of speech and hearing but eyes and facial muscles, hands and arms, brain and in many respects the entire body. Putting it more personally, communication is a holistic concept. It always involves the *whole* of you: mind and heart, body and spirit.

Ask yourself
Do I seek to avoid confusion in the mind of the other person by ensuring that my body language always supports the intent and content of what I say?

Idea 7: Communication and relationships

The bird carries the wings, but the wings carry the bird.

Chinese saying

Sustained communication between individuals tends to lead to the formation of some sort of relation between them. Conversely, the better the relation between two people the more communication – in all its width, depth and height – becomes possible between them. This is another fundamental principle.

The key ingredient here is *trust.* Trust between people is a confident reliance on or belief in the integrity, veracity, justice, power or protection of a person or thing.

The Old Norse word *traust* from which we derive trust is also related to *tryggr*, true. As it suggests, truth and trust are inseparably linked in the business of creating and maintaining close human relations.

If you consistently do not speak the truth, then you will do irreparable damage to any relationship between you and another person or persons. That in turn renders communication at first ever more problematic and then eventually impossible. Why should they ever listen to you again? 'Trust being lost,' wrote the Roman historian Livy, 'all human intercourse comes to naught.'

In summary: if you want to have good communication at work, as in your private life, you must build relationships. And you cannot do that without truth-orientated, two-way communication: listening as well as talking. The key ingredient in any human story is to breed trust or mutual confidence. And that is the by-product of both parties having the willingness and courage to be truthful.

*'When you break your word, you break something
that cannot be mended.'*

Idea 8: Feedback

When imparting a message of any kind to others, some of the energy you expend comes back to you in the form of feedback. You tell a joke and the audience laughs; you perform a song and the audience claps. That laughter and applause are forms of feedback.

The actual word *feedback*, now so common in everyday use, was coined by Norbert Wiener, an American applied mathematician and founder of cybernetics, in an influential book entitled *Cybernetics: Or Control and Communication in the Animal and the Machine* (1946).

In this seminal book Wiener compared communication to a system that loops back on itself: the parts are linked together in a cycle of activity like a child's electrical train set. Information does not just pass downwards or outwards, it curves backwards like a boomerang and affects the communicator. It was this phenomenon of bouncing back, the return of information through the system, that he called feedback. It is an expression of one of Newton's laws of motion, namely that every action will have a reaction.

As an effective communicator you should not only be aware that feedback will reach you sooner or later, but also be able to interpret it properly. There are, for example, many different kinds of laughter. Is your audience laughing *at* you or *with* you?

Look in the first instance for any feedback that indicates whether or not your message has been received and understood. A nod or smile may tell you as much; a blank look or puzzled expression is an invitation to try again.

> **Exercise**
>
> There were two sons who were ordered to do the same job by their father. The first expressed great willingness, with many nods and smiles, but he did nothing more about it.
>
> The second son said he was far too busy and could not possibly do it, but after second thoughts he went out and quietly did what his father had requested.
>
> What feedback was available to the father in both cases?

When your communication takes the form of an instruction to do something or to refrain from doing something, it is not the initial emotional response – be it positive or negative – that matters, but whether or not the action is done in the way you envisaged.

'Feedback is the food of champions.'

Idea 9: Accentuate the positives

None love the messenger that brings bad tidings.

Sophocles, Greek playwright

In almost any form of communication – meetings, interviews, public speaking – it is always good policy to start with a positive if you possibly can. It might be a short word of thanks or repeating something that is already known, but it really can smooth the way for a productive meeting. A negative start always produces a negative response.

 Remind yourself

Try to find two or three positives to start off with. If you do have some blunt things to say that might be considered negative, always have ready a few solutions or creative ways forward so that you can end on a positive note.

Always bear this principle in mind if it falls to your lot to offer critical feedback or constructive advice to others. You and I are not the greatest people alive, I know, but we aren't completely useless: there are some positive things about us. Avoid those people who are colour blind to the positives in you. They only see the negatives, the shades of grey. They have nothing to contribute to you. They are drains of energy, not radiators.

'My glass is half full and tomorrow will be a better day.'

Idea 10: The Communication Star

A picture is worth a thousand words.

Chinese proverb

Communication is like a three-legged stool. In the basic model of a good conversation there are two people or parties engaged in a fundamentally two-way process of communication. The third element is that communication is always *about* something. So there are three elements: *speaker, listener* (which alternate) and *content*.

The Communication Star model clearly identifies those three factors.

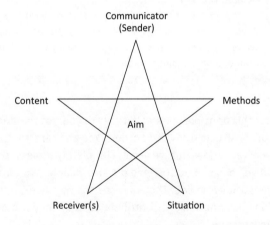

The Communication Star

You will see at a glance that there are three other elements in the picture: *aim*, *methods* and *situation*.

Aim   The intention of the message is the purpose in the sender's mind for sending it. It is the reason communication is taking place.

| **Methods** | How the message is conveyed. Writing, speaking or using signs are simple examples of methods. |
| **Situation** | The context or environment in which the communication is taking place. |

The aim or intention you have in mind, the methods you choose and the setting of the meeting all contribute positively or negatively to the outcome. If, for example, you are not clear about what you are trying to communicate, don't expect your 'receiver' to be clear. Would Lincoln's famous address on the battlefield of Gettysburg have sounded the same if it had been delivered in a baseball stadium?

Remind yourself
Always consider when you are planning the overall pattern of communication: all the points of the star in relation to the aim, never simply one element in isolation from all the others.

Idea 11: Important, relevant or interesting

The most important thing here is that there is no point in saying hello and addressing people if you don't have anything relevant, interesting or important to say. People will just either forget you or remember you for being the person who had nothing to say.

Deborah Meaden, British entrepreneur

Conversation, as opposed to the kind of talk that is called tittle-tattle or chatter, is always *about* something. And communication is conversation with its best clothes on.

Even the newsreader on television is engaged with you in a form of conversation about what is happening in the world today. Because of the nature of the method used, however, you are a silent partner in that conversation.

Notice that the editors in the newsroom select the stories that they judge to be *important*, *relevant* or *interesting* to their viewers taken as a whole.

Before you attempt to communicate in, say, a meeting or a presentation, I suggest that you follow the same path. Ask yourself these questions:

- ◆ In what ways is the content *important* to my audience? Of what consequence is it to them?
- ◆ How is it *relevant* to their work or their lives?
- ◆ Is it *interesting*? If it is not superficially so because of the nature of the subject, how can I make it interesting?

If you strike that chord of three notes, or two at the very least, on the sounding board of your audience's mind, you will be rewarded by their lively, sympathetic or curious attention. That is the secret of creating a listener.

Ask yourself
Before speaking, do I always double-check that what I have to offer is important, relevant or interesting?

Idea 12: Active listening

Listen to all, pluck a feather from every passing goose, but follow no one absolutely.

Chinese proverb

In a good conversation both parties will talk and both will listen. In more formal contexts, however, one person may be cast more in the role of speaker and the other people are likewise more in the role of listeners. The actors in a theatre, for example, are clearly the speakers and the audience the listening part of the company.

Because listeners tend not to speak much it is often assumed that listening is a rather passive business. Not so. A good listener will give their active and thoughtful attention to the speaker. Their mutual aim is to ensure that what is in the speaker's mind *does* really become common property.

Listening requires entering actively and imaginatively into the other fellow's situation and trying to understand a frame of reference different from your own. This is not always an easy task.

S.I. Hayakawa, *Language in Thought and Action (1949)*

Notice that there is no implication that the active listener should necessarily *agree* with the speaker. Whether or not you accept what they say or do as they request is always a secondary issue. The first requirement is to be clear what they mean.

To become a truly excellent communicator, you must invest as much time and energy in becoming an excellent listener as you do in endeavouring to become a first-class speaker.

'Examine what is said, not the person saying it.'

Idea 13: The wonder of languages

You are as many a person as languages you know.

Armenian proverb

Language is the principal means of personal communication, both in its oral and written forms. So it is worth reflecting on this marvellous human creation, the greatest legacy we owe to our forebears.

All languages have evolved to perform the same function, but they sound and look very different. Each is a key to an experience of the world, in many respects common to yours or mine. Thus we can more or less accurately translate one language into another, but each language also reflects a unique culture.

The practical implication is that if you want to communicate effectively in any language, your native one or an acquired language, you should appreciate its peculiar strengths and weaknesses, the mirror of its usually long history.

Equally, however, you should seek to understand the natural language of those with whom you are communicating, especially its frames of reference. Remember, too, that if they can speak your language it is not necessarily the case that they will understand the frames of reference – the nuances or overtones behind words – that you take for granted.

Once I asked a Finnish audience to discuss in groups of two or three the differences between being a manager and being a leader.

They looked at me blankly, but did as I requested. Only later did I learn that in Finnish the same word means both leader and manager!

Case study

One of the world's 2,400 endangered languages is a Tibetan-Burman one, spoken in the Thangmi community.

The Thangmi lexicon is pretty compact, with just over 2,000 'words', and not always ones that we would expect. For example, while there are no Thangmi terms for 'village', 'table', 'left' or 'right', there are specific verbs to mean 'to be exhausted by sitting in the sun all day' and 'to be infested with lice', as well as precise nouns to describe edible parts of certain leaves or particularly chewy meat that gets stuck in one's teeth.

In other words, things that are culturally salient and meaningful to its speakers.

'Language is more than words, it is about how people experience and think about life.'

Idea 14: Seven rules for becoming a great communicator

1. Examine the true purpose of each communication. Always ask yourself what you really want to accomplish with your message.

2. Be mindful, while you communicate, of the overtones as well as the basic content of your message.

3. When it comes to content, bear in mind the enduring value of truth in any human communication. As one Ethiopian proverb says: 'Over truth there is light.'

4. Consider the total physical and human setting whenever you communicate. Check your sense of *timing* against the situation. There is a time and a place for everything.

5. Take the opportunity, when it arises, to convey something of help or value to the receiver.

6. Be sure that your actions support your communication. Words should interpret what is done and action should accompany words. Eventually our words should become acts and our acts our truest words.

7. Seek not only to be understood but also to understand – be a good listener.

Follow-up test

Understanding communication

☐ Would you agree that the core of communication is *sharing*, the making common of what is in the mind of one person so that others may share it as fully as the speaker or writer?

☐ Can you think of three examples in your working life where misunderstandings have arisen out of different interpretations of the same word or phrase?

☐ Do you encourage two-way communication in your team and in your organization?

☐ As far as possible, do you model your communication on the kind of conversation that is purposeful, in the sense that both parties want to explore something together?

☐ Do people sometimes misinterpret your body language, reading into it messages that you do not intend?

☐ As a leader, do you make sure that your body language expresses a positive attitude?

☐ Do you always make building trust your top priority in forming professional or personal relationships?

☐ Which of these statements best describes your own policy?
  1. 'I trust people until they show themselves to be untrustworthy.'
  2. 'I do not trust people until they demonstrate that they can be trusted.'

☐ Are you always aware of feedback when you are communicating messages or instructions to others?

☐ Do you read the non-verbal feedback, especially in people's faces, as well as the spoken or written word?

☐ Which comes first in your way of talking, the positives or the negatives?

☐ What are the six points of the Communication Star?

☐ Are you willing to work at improving your communication skills as a listener, so that you move from very good to excellent?

PART TWO
Effective Speaking and the Art of Listening

The major mistake in communication is to believe that it happens.

George Bernard Shaw, Irish playwright

The art of communication is essentially a practical one. It includes skills such as *speaking, listening, writing* and *reading*, which we all do, but which few do excellently. Skills can all be improved by study and practice working together, hand in hand.

In practical communication the first two, the oral skills, take precedence over their two literary siblings. Thus the focus of Part Two is on *effective speaking* and the *art of listening*.

Don't think of effective speaking as being only about public speaking, the sort of talk you may be asked to do at a wedding or other formal occasion. As a manager you will be speaking all day: at team meetings, on the telephone, at one-to-one meetings, at conferences with colleagues or clients. The six principles of effective speaking are relevant to all these situations.

You will also be doing a lot of listening at work. Part Two raises the bar for you as a listener. Don't aim to be a good listener – that's too easy. Don't even aim to be a very good listener, rare as they are. Go for gold!

Like learning a new language, your conscious efforts to study and practise the principles in Part Two may seem awkward and full of mistakes at first. But that is to be expected, for art lies in perfecting our natural gifts. Eventually these efforts will drift into the subconscious mind and continue to influence your attitudes and actions without you being aware that they are doing so. And one day people will say that you are a 'born communicator'. Little do they know!

After a concert an enthusiastic member of the audience came up to the great violinist Fritz Kreisler and said, 'I would give my life to play the violin like you did this evening.'

'I did,' replied Kreisler.

Twenty-four Greatest Ideas for Effective Speaking

Idea 15: Six principles of effective speaking

Occasions for public speaking abound. In our working lives we may have to give briefings or talks, take part in presentations or even deliver formal lectures. The good news is that *you don't have to be a great orator.*

Given that you have something important, relevant or interesting to impart, there are six key principles you need to master in order to become a really effective speaker. Apply them consistently and with practice you will have no problems with effectiveness as a speaker, I promise you.

1. *Be clear.*
   This is the golden rule for all communicators. What is clarity? A clear sky is one free of clouds, mists and haze. With reference to speech it means a complete freedom from any form of confusion and hence communicating something that is easy to grasp and understand. Being clear is not primarily a matter of your sentences or words, it is a product of your mind. As an inner principle, it starts at source, with the thoughts in your head.
2. *Be prepared.*
   Preparation calls for active, conscious deliberation and efforts *before* the action happens. To be unprepared, by contrast, means that you have not thought about or made any attempt at readying yourself for what you know you may or will have to face. You are like a football team that never trains or plans before its matches.
3. *Be simple.*
   Don't put off your listeners by offering them something that is unnecessarily complicated or intricate. But don't

oversimplify or talk down to your audience, even if they happen to be children.

4. *Be vivid.*
    Make what you say come alive! This graphic or colourful quality springs from the commitment, interest or enthusiasm in the mind and heart of you, the communicator. But it has to be reflected in your language as well.

5. *Be natural.*
    Be natural or, if you prefer it, be yourself – your best self. What you say and how you say it should reflect your own personality.

6. *Be concise.*
    Be economical with your words and other people's time. Less is more.

'It is easier to speak than actually to say something.'

Idea 16: The importance of preparation

If I had eight hours to chop down a tree I'd spend six hours sharpening my axe.

US President Abraham Lincoln

You need to prepare yourself well in advance for occasions when you know you have to make a speech of some kind or another. You may have weeks or only a few minutes at your disposal, but the principle of preparation is still applicable.

While the manner or degree of preparation you can achieve will vary considerably, it is useful to distinguish between *general preparation* and *particular preparation*.

General preparation

Think of the example of a portrait painter. Most, if not all, of your training and experience will have equipped you for the moment when you actually paint a portrait, as illustrated by this case study.

Particular preparation

Particular preparation covers what soldiers would call the tactics of the situation. For the portrait artist it means such activities as putting primer on the canvas, selecting and arranging the brushes and paints and making sure that the studio is warm and well lit. It may have already included some reflection on the personality or character of the sitter who is coming that day: what music they may like to listen to, what they like to talk about or what refreshments to offer them.

Fail to prepare and you prepare to fail.

Case study: Sir Joshua Reynolds

The famous portrait painter Sir Joshua Reynolds, first President of the Royal Academy, once painted the portrait of a successful iron magnate, a self-made man of immense wealth. Like many rich men he was careful with his money. When he received the invoice for some hundreds of guineas, a great sum in those days, he exploded with anger and walked over to Sir Joshua's studio to complain.

'You spent no more than 12 hours on my face,' he declared, 'and your assistants did most of the work on the rest of me. Why charge me over £600 for 12 hours' work? I wouldn't pay my best manager that sum.'

'You are not paying me for 12 hours, Sir,' replied Reynolds. 'You are paying me for over 30 years in which I learned with much toil and trouble what to do with my brushes in those 12 hours.'

Ask yourself
How can I apply the principle of preparation in my line of work?

Idea 17: A simple checklist for planning

I keep six honest serving-men
(They taught me all I knew);
Their names are What and Why and When
And How and Where and Who.

Rudyard Kipling, 'The Elephant Child'
in the *Just So Stories* (1902)

Kipling here gives you a simple and easy-to-remember checklist to use whenever you are called on to make a speech of any kind. These are the six keys that unlock the door and enable you to prepare and plan with confidence.

Question	Action
Who?	Who are you going to communicate to? Try to visualize an individual, several people or an audience. What are their interests, presuppositions and values? What do they share in common with others? How are they unique?
What?	What do you wish to communicate? One way of answering this question is to ask yourself about the 'success criteria'. How will you know if and when you have successfully communicated what you have in mind?
How?	How can you best convey your message? Language is important here. Choose your words with the audience in mind. Plan a beginning, middle and end. If time and place allow them, consider and prepare some audio-visual aids.
When?	Timing is all important in communication. Develop a sense of timing, so that your contributions are seen and heard as relevant to the issue or matter in hand. There is a time to speak and a time to be silent. 'It is better to be silent than to sing a bad tune.'

Question	Action
Where?	What is the physical context of the communication? You may have time to visit the room, for example, and rearrange the furniture. Check for audibility (and visibility if you are using visual aids).
Why?	There is a world of difference between an audience who hears what you say, and one that listens to what you are saying. In order to convert 'hearers' into listeners you need to know why they should listen to you – and tell them if necessary. What disposes them to listen? This implies that you yourself know why you are seeking to communicate and know the value, worth or interest of what you are going to say.

Idea 18: Be clear

What is conceived well is expressed clearly,
And words to say it will arise with ease.

Nicholas Boileau, French poet and critic

Clear thinking manifests itself in a clear utterance: if your thoughts or ideas are a bit confused, vague or fuzzy, then they will be that much less easily understood or perceived.

Clarity is the cardinal principle of power or effectiveness in both speech and writing. Therefore good communication begins in the mind. Thus the application of this principle has to begin a long way back from the boardroom or executive office. It begins in the struggle to achieve clarity in the uncertain weather of your mind. It entails using your intellectual skills of analyzing, synthesizing and valuing to ensure that what you have to say is crystal clear. Whether or not your hearers accept what you say is, strictly speaking, a secondary issue; the primary requirement is that they should understand it as clearly as you do.

Ask yourself
Can I think of three speakers in different fields who have demonstrated to me the principle of being clear?

Idea 19: A master of clear speaking

Stars shine always in a clear sky.

Estonian proverb

When I was a pupil at St Paul's School I was fortunate to sit at the feet of a master of the art of being clear. Field Marshal Lord Montgomery, who happened to be an ex-pupil of the school, came back to give a lecture to the sixth form about the campaign that led up to the famous victory of El Alamein in the Second World War.

Monty, as he was universally known, had based the Allied Headquarters responsible for the planning of D-Day and the invasion of Nazi-occupied Europe in the large red brick building that his old school had vacated for the duration.

Thus he spoke to us in the very same lecture hall that he had used for his final briefings on those plans to King George VI, Winston Churchill and General Eisenhower. It was easy for me as a schoolboy to capture the 'atmosphere', as Montgomery liked to call it.

Above all, his refreshing clarity lingers in my mind, as well as the fact that he spoke without notes – something that I learned to do myself much later.

He could describe a complex situation with amazing lucidity and sum up a long exercise without the use of a single note. He looked straight into the eyes of the audience when he spoke. He had a remarkable flair for picking out the essence of a problem, and for indicating its solution with startling clarity. It was almost impossible to misunderstand his meaning, however unpalatable it might be.

If you want to achieve that enviable clarity, the arrangement or structure of what you are saying should be clear, so that people know roughly where they are and where they are going. The reasoning should be sharp and clean cut, without the blurred edges of those who gloss over the issues.

Lastly, avoid the obscure reference, the clouded remark, the allusion that few will understand or the word that is fashionable but all too muddy in its meaning.

Idea 20: In praise of simplicity

Everything should be made as simple as possible but not more simple.

Albert Einstein, German physicist

In order to communicate effectively you first need something to impart to others that is, within your shared context, *important*, *relevant* or *interesting*. That is only an indicative list. In some contexts, for example, you can add *instructive* or *entertaining*.

What you have to say in a given field of knowledge – think of musicology, pure mathematics or subatomic physics – may be so complex, so couched in a special sublanguage of symbols, that only a fellow professional at your level will be able to understand what you are talking about. But even in these contexts the instinct of the born communicator – like the great composer, mathematician or physicist – is always to aim for the maximum simplicity that the situation allows. We have Einstein as our authority here.

Simple stresses singleness of character and is distinguished from what is *compound* or *complex*. It suggests that something cannot be analyzed or reduced further. Einstein, however, warns us against being *oversimple* or simplistic. For simple as applied to abstractions or conceptions often suggests a false or artificial freedom from complexity. Oversimplification implies that certain essential factors may have been eliminated, which in turn undermines the message.

In Greek legend Procrustes was a robber of Attica, who placed all who fell into his hands on an iron bed. If they were longer than the bed he cut off the overhanging parts, if shorter he stretched them until they fitted it. Hence any attempt to reduce people to one standard, one way of thinking or one way of acting, is called 'placing them on Procrustes' bed'.

True simplicity is achieved by the best minds in any field *after* they have immersed themselves in the complexities of their subject, not before. It never compromises on those essential factors. That is why simplicity is the brother or sister of truth.

Idea 21: First, think through what you want to say

What can be said at all can be said clearly.

Ludwig Wittgenstein, Austrian philosopher

Finding the true simplicity in your professional field's body of knowledge should be one of the key objects of your own thinking and study. If you can achieve that, then one of the rewards is that you will have greatly enhanced your power to communicate to others.

Willy Brandt, former Chancellor of what was then West Germany, said of Jean Monnet, the father of the Common Market that led to today's European Union: 'He had the ability to put complicated matters into simple formulae.' Doubtless in politics simplicity is a sign of statesmanship, just as it accompanies outstanding ability in the arts and sciences.

Exercise

Take a little time to answer the following questions. They should help to provide some clarity on the concept of being simple:

◆ Can you think of someone in your professional field who has the gift of making complex matters sound simple without talking down or becoming simplistic?

◆ Choose one aspect of your work that is by universal consent not easy for a layperson to understand. How would you explain it to a group of hunter-gatherer South American Indians through an interpreter?

◆ List three reasons why professional people sometimes deliberately choose to take an essentially simple subject in their field and make it sound as complicated as possible.

Remind yourself

Being simple means that your hearers will not be put off by words that are unnecessarily complicated or intricate. But don't oversimplify or talk down to your audience, even if they are children.

Idea 22: Don't overload your speech

When you speak to an audience there is always a time constraint – or there should be! You share an allocation of so much time and no more.

Therefore you have to be very clear about your intention or aim and what priorities that dictates for your material. Don't overload the hold of your aircraft with so much unnecessary freight that you never get off the runway.

And avoid giving your listeners undue difficulties. In this context, *simple* refers to something that is not complicated or intricate and is therefore capable of being quickly grasped by the mind. It should not be confused with *easy*, which merely points to that which requires little effort to do.

The search for simplicity in thinking is the same as the search for the essence of a subject, that which is specific to it and not composite or mixed up with other matters. Such a quest demands skills of analysis.

You have to dissect, discard, blow away and burn off before you isolate the essential simplicity of a subject. To simplify means to render less intricate or difficult and thus capable of being more easily understood, performed or used.

Keep it simple

Former British Prime Minister Harold Macmillan once related how after his maiden speech in the Commons, his legendary predecessor David Lloyd George – one of the great political orators of the twentieth century – asked him to come to see him.

Lloyd George complimented Macmillan on his first attempt and then gave him a tip:

If you are an ordinary Member of Parliament, make only one point in your speech (you can make it in different ways but it should centre on one point). If you are a minister, you may make two. Only if you are a Prime Minister can you afford to make three points.

That discipline of making just one, two or three points – depending on the time available and the demands of the situation – is worth bearing in mind. It compares to the principle of conciseness. And let the point you are making be clear; do not drown it in words.

Remind yourself
Honest, plain talk is the reward for simplicity, not the means to it. The distinction may seem slight, but it is tremendously important.

Idea 23: Use everyday language

Think as wise men do, but speak as the common people do.

Aristotle, Greek philosopher

The ability to speak simply about difficult subjects without oversimplification is one of the marks of an effective speaker. We should certainly not fall into the trap of equating simplicity with being simplistic or superficial. What is simple may have depth, just as sophistication may disguise emptiness. Above all, don't lose yourself and your audience in a maze of complications, real or imagined.

One reason some speakers choose to use jargon – any professional, technical or specialized language – is because they don't understand one of the basic principles of communication, namely that *both* parties need to share the same frame of reference and set of common symbols (which here means vocabulary).

Another and perhaps more common reason is that the speaker wishes to impress the listener or audience with their knowledge or learning or importance. The best speakers don't do that, even with their fellow professionals. 'I'm allowed to use plain English because everybody knows that I could use mathematical logic if I chose,' wrote logician and philosopher Bertrand Russell in *Portraits from Memory* (1956).

In fact, if you *are* an expert or specialist you don't need to tell your audience that fact, least of all by self-consciously trying to display your expertise. Who you are conveys itself. As the Chinese proverb says, 'A tiger does not have to proclaim its tigerishness.'

In fact, good orators and writers have known for centuries the value of using the simple word. In Lincoln's Gettysburg address, of the total of 268 words, 190 have only one syllable.

Idea 24: How the best leaders communicate

Speak properly, and in as few words as you can, but always plainly; for the end of speech is not ostentation, but to be understood.

William Penn, social reformer and founder of Pennsylvania

If you wish to communicate effectively you have to do so in the language and thought idioms of your audience. This principle is especially important for you as a leader. You want your hearers not only to understand you but also to take action in the way you want. To that end, you have to be able to inspire people while you inform them.

Writing to Lady Hamilton in October 1805 from HMS *Victory*, Lord Nelson described the reaction of his captains to the strategy he outlined for the impending Battle of Trafalgar:

I joined the Fleet late on the evening of the 28th but could not communicate with them until the next morning. I believe that my arrival was most welcome, not only to the Commander of the Fleet, but also to every individual in it; and when I came to explain to them the 'Nelson touch', it was like an electric shock. Some shed tears, all approved – 'It was new – it was singular – it was simple!' and, from Admirals downwards, it was repeated – 'It must succeed, if ever they will allow us to get at them.'

Nelson had the advantage that he had been in the Royal Navy since the age of twelve. He understood not only the language of sailors, including all the jargon, but also how sailors thought.

Ask yourself

Am I putting across what I want to say in plain English or its equivalent in my own language?

Idea 25: Learn the common frame of reference

The king-becoming graces,
As justice, verity, temperance, stableness,
Bounty, perseverance, mercy, lowliness,
Devotion, patience, courage, fortitude.

William Shakespeare, Macbeth

In his plays Shakespeare explored leadership in its contemporary form, kingship. In those days, as his sovereign Queen Elizabeth I acknowledged, kings were expected to lead from the front in battle.

For Shakespeare the king who exemplified these 'king-becoming graces' – or leadership qualities – was Henry *VI*, victor at the battle of Agincourt and conqueror of most of France. The secret of his success, Shakespeare hinted, was the rapport he established with the youths of London, his future soldiers, while he was not yet their king.

As Prince Hal, but with his real name and identify kept secret, he frequented the taverns in East London used by the young apprentices. As one observer (in *Henry IV*, Part I, Act 4) described him at work:

The prince but studies his companions
Like a strange tongue, wherein to gain the language.
'Tis needful that the most immodest word
Be look'd upon and learn'd.

Prince Hal soon acquired what he came to learn. He said:

To conclude, I am not so good a proficient in one quarter of an hour, that I can drink with any tinker in his own language during my life.

The incognito prince found that he could be accepted on the apprentices' terms, as if he was one of them. A leader is among the people, not over them.

> *They take it already upon their salvation, that though I be but Prince of Wales, yet I am the king of courtesy . . . a lad of mettle, a good boy, by the Lord, so they call me! And when I am King of England, I shall command all the good lads in Eastcheap.*

In the play *Henry VI,* there are some long and eloquent speeches by the king, not least a famous one before the advance to the decisive attack at Agincourt, but that is Shakespeare speaking. History does record two versions of what Henry actually said at that critical moment. The more laconic version is just three words: 'Fellows, let's go.'

Remind yourself
To communicate as a leader you need to speak to your people in their own language.

Idea 26: Make it live for your audience

A flame should be lighted at the commencement and kept alive with unremitting splendour to the end.

Michael Faraday, English chemist and author
of *Advice to a Lecturer*

If you cannot interest your audience in what you are saying you are dead as a speaker. How do you capture and hold the interest of an audience?

The first rule, of course, is to be interested yourself in what you are talking about and the people to whom you are talking – in that order. And you have to communicate that double interest to your audience with enthusiasm.

Enthusiasm, however quiet and unassuming, is your ace card. Your audience will find it hard to resist your enthusiasm in the content of your speech, which is your interest blazing and crackling with happy flames. It is extremely difficult for an enthusiastic speaker to be dull, so take courage.

The wider principle of vividness (see Idea 15) covers all that goes to make what you say interesting, arresting and attractive. From the Latin verb *vivere* meaning 'to live', the word vivid literally translates as 'full of life'.

Remind yourself

Make what you say come alive! This graphic or colourful quality springs from the interest and enthusiasm in the mind and heart of you, the communicator. But it has to become visible in your language.

Idea 27: Eight tips for using humour

Wit is the salt of conversation, not the food.

William Hazlitt, English essayist

If as a businessperson you are a frequent flyer, you know how we all tend to be only half-listening when the air crew begin to recite the safety instructions. Once, however, my ears suddenly pricked up. 'There may be 50 ways to leave your lover,' the steward said, 'but there are only five ways to leave this aircraft.' And then: 'Please return your seat to its upright and most uncomfortable position. Later you may lean back and break the knees of the passenger behind you.'

The story makes a serious point: humour can grab someone's attention and help to get your message across. Some people can't tell a joke to save their lives, but everyone can learn to use humour effectively. The secret is to develop your own style, learn a few tricks and take time to practise. Here are eight practical tips:

1. Work out whether you are better with stories or one-liners. Don't try to be what you are not.
2. Look for material from your own experience. One day I asked my 10-year old daughter if she thought I was a leader. She considered for rather too long a time, and then replied: 'Yes, Daddy, you are a leader – but Mummy's the boss.'
3. Nothing puts people more at ease than self-deprecating humour. 'Why do people call me a guru?' Peter Drucker once asked, before answering: 'Because it's shorter than charlatan!'
4. Humour should be adapted to the audience. The more pertinent and specific the humour, the funnier it is.

5. Avoid humour that implies criticism of your audience or some part of it; you may be cutting rather too close to the bone. Only tease people about matters that they joke about among themselves.

6. Forget the old formula that a speech should open and close with a joke: that kind of routine only signals insecurity on your part.

7. If you do use an opening joke or story, it should have a strong point that will set up the entire speech.

8. Keep your humorous aside short and tell it slowly. No matter how amusing they are to you, don't laugh at your own jokes while you're telling them.

 Remind yourself

Humour, it has been said, is 'a warm-hearted, sympathetic and good-natured treatment of small failings or ironies'. It usually prompts smiles rather than people's laughter. You are not in the business of being a stand-up comedian.

Idea 28: Truth through personality

You make the audience say, 'How well he speaks!' I make them say, 'Let us march against Philip!'

Demosthenes, the greatest of all Athenian orators

As the speaker, it is within your power to capture and direct the attention of your audience. That attention should be firmly attached to the content of what you want to say, not to you or your personality. If you are wise, you won't make your speech an ego trip.

You cannot, of course, eliminate personality altogether, even if you were so foolish as to want to do so. Whatever light we have to bring to dispelling some of the fuzziness around us always comes through the lens of personality.

You should, however, strive to keep your lens clear of any of those kinds of imperfections that may distract the attention of the audience away from the business in hand and towards you as an individual person.

Like the greatest artists and performers, great leaders at all levels are essentially self-effacing. They are not concerned with self or their image or how they personally are being perceived. They are focused on the work in hand. 'I prefer to think how arms, legs and head are attached to the body than whether I am or am not more or less an artist,' wrote Vincent Van Gogh to his brother. And yet it is not difficult for most people to recognize a painting by Van Gogh.

What you are will come across naturally and of its own accord. Centre yourself on the truth you want to convey, and your personality will find its own way to a listener's mind and heart.

Idea 29: Leadership and communication

Not the cry but the flight of the wild duck leads the flock to fly and to follow.

Chinese proverb

Leadership and communication are closely linked. It is impossible to think of a good leader who is not a good communicator.

Leaders are sometimes told that first and foremost they should be servants of their people. Not so. As J.B. Yeats wrote from New York in 1944 in a letter to his son, the poet W.B. Yeats:

> *The real leader serves truth, not people, not his followers, and he cares little for authority or for the exercise of power, excepting so far as they help him to serve truth, and we follow him because we too, when your attention is directed to it, would also serve truth, that being a fundamental law of human nature – however unfaithful to it we may often be when misled by passion or self-interest.*

Such leaders, continued Yeats, gain a ready audience:

> *Their command excites no anger, since we are not brought face to face with an Ego. They and all of us are serving a mistress [the truth] who really issues the orders we obey.*

The Eastern tradition of leadership, which reaches back to Confucius and Lao Tzu in the 6th century BCE, echoes what Yeats says. For it presents as an ideal the self-effacing leader; in sharp contrast, it must be added, to the more egotistical Western models still so prevalent today. The leader is a humble servant of truth, content to let the credit for accomplishing the common task go to others; that's the badge of humility.

A leader is best when he is neither seen nor heard. Not so good when he is adored and glorified. Worst when he is hated and despised. 'Fail to honour people, they will fail to honour you.' But of a great leader, when his work is done, his aim fulfilled, the people will all say, 'We did this ourselves.'

Lao Tzu, Chinese Taoist philosopher

Ask yourself
How is it for me: truth or ego?

Idea 30: Truth, the greatest communicator of all

Truth has such a face and such a mien,
As to be loved needs only to be seen.

John Dryden, *The Hind and the Panther* (1687)

I won't try to define truth, for no one can. Call it a value, if you like. If so, it is a universal one. 'We have an idea of truth, invincible to all scepticism,' wrote French mathematician, physicist and religious philosopher Blaise Pascal. Or, as Shakespeare put it in more homely language, 'Truth is truth, to the end of reckoning.'

Truth – the truth of the content or material, which becomes the common focus of attention – is immensely important in communication. It is the star that every good communicator steers by. You can command all the media, you can know all the tricks and techniques in the textbooks on communication skills, but if what you are saying is a lie in some degree, shape or form, it all adds up to nothing. Why? Because as people we are naturally oriented towards truth, goodness and beauty.

If you do manage to say something that is true, whatever the context or the level, you have a great advantage on your side. Truth communicates of its own accord. You will have to dress up a lie, disguise the truth, garnish it with bribes and incentives, in order to get it swallowed by your audience. Some politicians become experts in this black art. The truth, however, requires no such presentation. It speaks for itself.

> *'The language of truth is simple.'*

Idea 31: Avoid inaccuracies and exaggeration

There would be too great a darkness if truth had no visible signs.

Blaise Pascal, French mathematician and philosopher

In science you cannot prove that something is true; what you can do, however, is prove that theories are *not* true by subjecting them to a controlled series of experiments.

You can apply this principle of falsification more generally. You may not, for example, be able to convince people directly that what you are saying is true. But you can certainly avoid communicating to them something that is *not* true. Here are two useful habits.

Avoid inaccuracies

Few people set out to say things they know are incorrect, but errors have a way of creeping in to what you say or write and, unchecked, they can threaten your credibility. Accuracy calls for you to be precise; that is, to be in accordance with the truth.

Eighteenth-century English author Samuel Johnson advised:

> *Accustom your children constantly to this. If a thing happened at one window and they when relating it say it happened at another, do not let it pass but instantly check them.* You do not know where deviation from Truth will end.

That's good advice for all communicators.

Don't exaggerate

It is always tempting for a speaker or writer to heighten what they say for effect, to overstate it a little and then a little bit more, or to represent the situation as worse than is in fact the case. But strictly speaking such exaggeration, however justifiable as a means to an end, is a departure from the truth. It is another form of inaccuracy and you are straying into dangerous territory. If it is a humorous way of making a point, that's fine. But if you fall into the habit of exaggerating you will lose credibility. Is it worth it?

> *'Truth, the whole truth and nothing but the truth.'*

Idea 32: The ethics of communication

A lie stands on one leg, but truth upon two.

English proverb

The ethics of communication revolve around the issue of telling the truth. When is it permissible to lie? There are some common-sense occasions, as Samuel Johnson once explained:

> *The general rule is that truth should never be violated, because it is of the utmost importance for the comfort of life that we should have a full security by mutual faith, and occasional inconveniences should be willingly suffered that we may preserve it.*
>
> *There must, however, be some exceptions. If, for instance, a murderer should ask you which way a man is gone, you may tell him what is not true, because you are under a previous obligation not to betray a man to a murderer.*

Setting aside such an obvious exception – and the more taxing ones that may come to your mind – a useful principle to bear in mind is this one: *You need not tell all the truth, unless it is to those who have a right to know. But let all you tell be truth.*

In any case, it is usually unwise to share all your knowledge with another person. As the American jazz saxophonist James Brown said of his contemporaries, 'I taught them everything they know, but not everything I know.'

 Remind yourself
The faintest of all human passions is the love of truth.

Idea 33: How to become natural

Many things – such as loving, going to sleep or behaving unaffectedly – are done worst when we try hardest to do them.

C.S. Lewis, author of *The Chronicles of Narnia*

When you stand up to speak, the eyes of other people – possibly hundreds or even thousands – will be on you. Humans tend to find that experience uncomfortable, if not quite threatening. It takes time and practice before you can learn to relax and be yourself in the goldfish bowl of attention.

The experience is not unique to public speaking. We all know how difficult it can be to act naturally in certain circumstances. We should think nothing of jumping a four-foot-wide stream, but a similar gap several thousand feet up on a mountain can make us freeze with nerves.

The principle of being natural invites you to shut off the danger signals from the situation and speak as naturally as if you were standing in your own room at home. Easier said than done. Yet the art of relaxing can help to fight off a strained voice. The natural manners of experienced television entertainers give us plenty of models for observation.

The principle of naturalness is not, however, a licence to be your own worst self before a captive audience. Relaxation can so easily slip into sloppiness, just as 'doing what comes naturally' may be sometimes rightly interpreted by the audience as an inconsiderate lack of adequate preparation. Nor should you resort to friendly mumbling or inconsequential chatter, laced with 'you knows'.

Roman politician Cicero's definition of an orator was 'a good man skilled in speaking'. When it comes to public speaking, art – like all grace – should not destroy nature but perfect it.

Remind yourself
Stop thinking of yourself. Think only of your subject and your audience.

Idea 34: Don't worry about your voice or gestures

Do the thing you fear, and the death of fear is certain.

Ralph Waldo Emerson, American essayist

Many of the textbooks on communication devote a great deal of space to the techniques of breathing, intonation, pronunciation and gesturing. Doubtless there is much to be learned here, but it is possible to overstress the importance of these elocutionary actions.

Beyond the essentials of clear and distinct speech there is little that must be said. Variety in tone and pitch stem from one's natural interest and enthusiasm. If they are 'put on' or practiced in front of the mirror, the result can seem self-conscious and even theatrical – in a word, unnatural.

Being natural should not be equated with vocal relaxation, however. It includes giving expression in our speech to the natural emotions that human flesh is heir to.

For many of us, our education and culture teach us to suppress any public display of emotion and this can make communication sound stilted and artificial.

It is unfashionable for orators to weep in public nowadays, although Winston Churchill brushed the odd tear from his eye on more than one occasion. But naturalness follows if we allow the emotions of the moment – interest, curiosity, anger or passion – to colour our voices and our movements.

Yet they should serve the voice and not master it. 'I act best when my heart is warm and my head cool,' declared the American actor Joseph Jefferson, a sound principle for anyone who speaks to an audience.

If you *think* out what you are going to say – think it out over and over again, make a few notes and then trust that the words you need will come to mind – your performance will be human and natural. True, your talk may be a little halting in spots, your phraseology may not be perfect, and you are almost certain to leave out some of the things you intended to say; but what you do say will get over far better and more naturally than a memorized oration.

You may ask what gestures you should make. As far as the audience is concerned, it won't be necessary to make any gestures. But gestures may help *you* to let yourself go. Nevertheless, don't plan them in advance. You ought to be thinking only of your ideas, your message and your audience.

> *'Sincerity gives colour to your voice.'*

Idea 35: Be concise

Be brief, be sincere, be seated.

US President Franklin D. Roosevelt

If clarity, simplicity and vividness describe the *quality* of what you say, and truth, beauty and goodness determine the *value* of what you say, conciseness is about the *quantity* dimension.

Essentially, conciseness means brevity of expression. In an age conscious of the value of time – 'time is money', as US Founding Father Benjamin Franklin said – and of time management, long-windedness is a short-cut to losing the interest of colleagues as well as customers or clients.

Your ability to confine weighty matters to a relatively small space in time calls for almost surgical skills of thought. As the Arab proverb says, 'Measure the cloth seven times before you cut your coat.'

The Latin verb *concidere*, meaning 'to cut short', lies behind the word 'concise'. You have to cut out all that is superfluous or elaborative when you speak. Aim at the ideal of using exactly as many words as are required to express what you have in mind, and no more. Don't let your expenditure of speech be too great for your income of ideas!

'The more you say, the less people remember.'

Idea 36: Not a crowd but individuals

A large audience can be intimidating, even to an experienced speaker. But when you think about your audience, think of them not as a mass of people but as a number of individual persons who have collected themselves together for the purpose of hearing you.

> *Many years ago in Indianapolis, an old preacher asked why I was so tense. 'Because,' I replied, 'there are 5,000 people out there expecting me to be helpful.'*
>
> *'No, there aren't,' he said. 'There's only one person, Charles. No one hears you as a crowd. Everyone hears you as an individual.'*
>
> Charles Templeton, *Canadian evangelist turned atheist*

As individuals we perceive things in different ways; we have different patterns of interests, needs and desires. Plan that your audience will all take home the same message, but allow for individuals to buy some things just for themselves.

Idea 37: How to handle the question-and-answer phase

To question a wise man is the beginning of wisdom.

German proverb

Whenever you speak in public there is usually some time made available for a question-and-answer session. Poor speakers regards this phase as a rather unnecessary optional extra, something to be got through as quickly as possible. In fact it is the most important part of your whole session. Remember, communication is dialogue.

Some practical tips:

 ◆ Make sure that you are clear what the questioner is asking.
 ◆ Keep your answer as brief as fullness allows – don't 'gild the lily' with unsolicited information.
 ◆ Allow the questioner to come back to you if they wish.
 ◆ If you can't answer the question, don't bluff. There may be someone else in the audience who can supply the answer.
 ◆ Be a good listener, giving the questioner your thoughtful attention and being genuinely open to what they have to say. As the Japanese say, 'To teach is to learn.'
 ◆ Be especially open to any critical or challenging remarks. Remind yourself that speaker and audience share a common aim: the truth. There is often a wisdom of crowds, so be a receiver as well as a giver.

Sometimes you can predict the questions you will be asked, but beware of losing spontaneity. A 'Q&A' session, or a period set aside for discussion, is really a test of your *general* preparation, how much you are a master of your profession or business. No wonder the ill-prepared fear this public examination!

> *'Authority flows from the one who knows.'*

Idea 38: Checklist – Putting the principles of communication to work

☐ 'You win the match before you run onto the field.' Do you believe that this sporting maxim applies to speaking?

☐ Do you take time to plan what you are going to say before and during meetings, interviews and telephone calls?

☐ Has anyone found anything you have said or written in the last week to be lacking in clarity?

☐ Have you taken steps to become a clear thinker?

☐ Which of these statements better describes you?

   ☐ 'He/she can make the complicated sound simple.'

   ☐ 'He/she tends to turn even the simplest matter into something that is difficult and complicated.'

☐ Are you an enthusiastic, interesting and lively speaker? (Tick the no box if the following words have been used about you, or anything you have said or written, in the last year: *dull, boring, lifeless, lacking creative spark, monotonous, flat* or *pedestrian*.)

☐ Do you think it is difficult to relax and be yourself when you are communicating?

☐ Have you a reputation for making concise oral contributions and writing succinct letters or memos?

☐ Do you find that you are beginning to enjoy the art of communication?

Six Greatest Ideas for the Art of Listening

Idea 39: The disease of not listening

Lord Chief Justice: You hear not what I say to you.

Falstaff: Very well, my Lord, very well; rather an't please you, it is the disease of not listening, the malady of not marking, that I am troubled withal.

William Shakespeare, *Henry IV*

People often confuse listening with hearing. But 'I hear what you say' is not always the same as 'I am listening to you'. The latter implies more than reception of the sounds, more even than reception of the message. It suggests a thoughtful attention and openness to the implications of what is being said.

In *Henry IV* Shakespeare makes the difference clear in the courtroom dialogue between that incorrigible old rogue Falstaff and the Lord Chief Justice. Many of us, like Falstaff, suffer from 'the disease of not listening'. All too often listening is regarded negatively, as what you do while you are awaiting your turn to talk.

We all 'turn a deaf ear', we refuse to listen, on certain occasions. But making a habit of it, succumbing to 'the disease of not listening', is to become mentally and intellectually deaf.

One of the world's most common proverbs – you'll find it in Latin, English, French, Italian and German – says as much: 'There are none so deaf as those who will not hear.'

Remind yourself
People have two eyes and two ears and only one tongue – which suggests that they ought to look and listen twice as much as they speak.

Idea 40: Four symptoms of a poor listener

Everybody wants to talk, few want to think,
and nobody wants to listen.

Anonymous

1. *Selective listening.*
   Selective listening means that we are programmed to turn a deaf ear to certain topics or themes.
      The danger in selective listening is that it can become habitual and unconscious: we become totally unaware that we only want to listen to certain people or a limited range of ego-boosting news, or that we are filtering and straining information.
2. *Persistent interrupting.*
   Persistent interrupting is the most obvious badge of the bad listener.
      Of course interrupting is an inevitable part of every-day conversation, springing from the fact that we can think faster than the other person can talk. So the listener can often accurately guess the end of a sentence or remark. The nuisance interrupter, however, either gets it wrong or else, even worse, they elbow in with a remark that shoots out the fact that they haven't been listening to the half-completed capsule of meaning.
3. *Avoiding the difficult or technical.*
   Such is our addiction to the clear, simple and vivid that none of us cares for the difficult, long and dull and we throw the towel in too soon.
      But what is at issue is not merely someone's ability as a speaker but our skill as a listener. If the path has to

be tortuous and uphill, the courageous listener will follow. The fainthearted or lazy listener gives up at the first obstacle.

4. *Criticizing the speaker's delivery or visual aids.*

In set-piece situations such as presentations, lectures or addresses, one way of expressing one's non-listening ability is to fasten on the speaker's delivery or the quality of their audio-visual aids. Some trick of pronunciation, an accent or impediment, involuntary movements or mannerisms: all these can be seized on as excuses for not listening to the meaning.

Alternatively the audio-visual aids, which like Hannibal's elephants can be a terror to their own side, can go on the rampage and distract a weak listener. It is hard to listen when the delivery is bad and the audio-visual aids are threatening to get out of control, but such occasions do sort out the hearers from the listeners.

> 'He who listens well, speaks well.'

Idea 41: Five key listening skills

'Is there, do you think, an art of speaking as of other things, if it is to be done skilfully and with profit to the hearer?'
'Yes.'
'And are all profited by what they hear, or only some among them? So that it seems there is an art of listening as well of speaking . . . To make a statue needs skill; to view a statue aright needs skill also.'

Epictetus, Greek Stoic philosopher

Be willing to listen	Wanting to listen comes first. In most contexts listening also requires an openness of mind, a willingness in principle to think or act differently.
Hear the message	Receiving clearly what is actually being said – not a penny more, not a penny less – is the next vital ingredient. There may be problems in physically hearing; if so, they have to be overcome. The issue at this stage is not whether or not you agree but whether you hear clearly what is being said.
Interpret the meaning	The meaning in question is the speaker's meaning. It may be clear and intelligible. The test is whether or not you can play back to the other person what it means in your own words in such a way that they accept it as accurate.
Evaluate carefully	You may want to suspend judgement so that you can use information or ideas for creative thinking purposes. But at some stage or other you will need to assess the worth or value of the content of what you have listened to. Is it true? Is it useful?
Respond appropriately	Communication is two way. A response is called for. It may be no more than applause – or even silence. But it is still a response, which will in turn be interpreted by the speaker. Make sure that you respond appropriately.

Remind yourself
To make a statue needs skill; to view a statue properly needs skill also.

Idea 42: How to become an eager listener

Every person is my superior in some way,
in that I learn from him or her.

Ralph Waldo Emerson, American essayist

You can't force yourself to listen to people. It is not a legal require-ment, punishable by a spell in prison. In most cultures it is considered polite to listen – or, at least, to look as if you are doing so. But how do you persuade yourself to *really* listen?

The trick, I suggest, is to convince yourself that virtually everyone you meet, whether it be on purpose or by accident, is your potential teacher, if only you can find out what they have to teach. Nor will they charge you a fee. Even a bore can teach you something – patience.

Always keep a pocketbook or some paper at hand so that you can take notes of any new ideas or information. The creative thinker knows that ideas are elusive and often quickly forgotten, so he or she pins them down with pencil and paper. Heed the Chinese proverb: 'The strongest memory is weaker than the palest ink.'

Konosuke Matsushita used to keep such a listener's notebook in his pocket. 'A person who can create ideas worthy of note,' he wrote, 'is a person who has learned much from others.'

You may be disappointed ninety-nine times, but the hundredth oyster you open will yield you its lustrous pearl. It may not exactly be a pearl of wisdom. But it will be something that strikes you as important, relevant or interesting, something that you can take away and make your own.

The best exemplar of this willingness to invest in listening that I have so far met was the Canadian magnate Lord Thomson of Fleet. In a commemorative article soon after his death, the editor of *The Times,* one of the newspapers then owned by Roy Thomson, described his passion for listening thus:

> *Roy was never interviewed by anyone who could match him in the eliciting of information. His interest was in the hope that the companion might add information to some current concern, or even reveal some world which Roy had not so far entered.*
>
> *One of the best-known women journalists in the United States spent some fascinated hours with him, and said: 'You can say I found him disarming in his simplicity . . . I was totally unprepared for his childlike curiosity about everything. He is full of questions on every imaginable subject. He pumps everyone dry which is enormously flattering. Small wonder he knows something about everything.'*

'Listen for ideas.'

Idea 43: Reflective listening

Know how to listen, and you will profit even from those who talk loudly.

Plutarch, Greek historian

Ask questions

'He who is afraid of asking is ashamed of learning', says a Danish proverb. Ask not only information-seeking questions but reflective ones as well, such as: 'Would it be true to say that you believe . . . ?'

Use *prods* and *open-ended questions* to draw people out, to encourage further exploration, to check facts and connections, to establish a way forward. Phrases beginning with 'tell me', 'so', 'how', 'what', 'when', 'where' and 'why' are more likely to get you somewhere than 'I this' and 'I that'.

Weigh your evidence

Assertions that such and such is the case or is true should always be examined. Some assertions may be self-evident truths, but a rational person requires grounds for accepting others. What grounds for acceptance are being offered? Are they compelling or conclusive?

Watch your assumptions

We tend to make assumptions that are both conscious and unconscious. It is difficult to think without making assumptions, but the unconscious ones in particular can easily lead us into misinterpreting what the other person is saying.

Jumping to conclusions – assuming that we know what someone is going to say or do – is one form that this takes. Can you think of others?

Share your response

Finally, feel free *to make suggestions*, *express opinions* and *offer solutions*, as long as it is in a timely, well-judged way. What you're having to judge is whether the moment has arrived when your contribution will be taken on board, not whether it's an opportunity to discharge yourself of a minor frustration. This is not a recipe for bland listening denuded of your own views, but for listening effectively and comfortably.

Idea 44: Checklist – Are you a born listener yet?

- [ ] Do you pay close attention when others are talking?
- [ ] When sitting next to someone you don't know at a meal, do you always seek to find an area of common interest?
- [ ] Do you believe that everyone has something to teach or share with you that has value for you – now or in the future?
- [ ] Can you set aside such factors as a person's personality, voice or delivery in order to find out what he or she knows?
- [ ] Are you a curious person, interested in people, ideas and things?
- [ ] Do you respond with a smile or nod or word of encouragement as the speaker is talking? Do you maintain good eye contact?
- [ ] Do you have a good awareness of your own prejudices, blind spots and assumptions and are you aware that they can create problems for you as a listener? Do you control them?
- [ ] Are you patient with people who have difficulty in expressing themselves?
- [ ] Do you keep an open mind regarding others' point of view?
- [ ] Do you listen for the speaker's emotional meaning as well as the content?
- [ ] Do you often reflect, restate or paraphrase what the speaker has said in order to make sure you have the correct meaning?

It is a secret known to but few of no small use in the conduct of life, that when you fall into a man's conversation, the first thing you should consider, whether he has a greater inclination to hear you, or that you should hear him.

Sir Richard Steele, Irish writer and
co-founder of *The Spectator*

Follow-up test

Effective speaking

☐ Which of the six principles of effective speaking is the one that you need to practise most?

☐ Do you always invest sufficient time in preparing well before you have to speak?

☐ Are you systematic about your planning?

☐ How many times in the last year have people commended you as a speaker for being clear?

☐ 'Everything should be made as simple as possible but not more simple.' Is that principle reflected in your professional or technical speaking?

☐ Do you avoid overloading your listeners with non-essential and irrelevant information?

☐ What is your record like for avoiding unnecessary jargon and academic abstractions?

☐ Have you made a conscious effort to learn the language – the frames of reference – of those you aspire to lead?

☐ Where appropriate, do you allow your enthusiasm to show through, giving life and vigour to your speech?

☐ Do you use the kind of humour that works best for you and your particular audience?

☐ What matters most to you: the truth you are trying to communicate or what your audience thinks about you?

☐ Do you let the truth speak for itself?

☐ Are you eager to avoid inaccuracies or misleading exaggerations in what you say or write?

☐ Can you relax and be yourself – your best self – on occasions when you are called up to say a few words?

☐ Have you a reputation for being brief and to the point?

☐ When you speak, do you have a sense of talking to each individual in the room as opposed to addressing a crowd?

The art of listening

☐ How far are you afflicted by the disease of not listening?

☐ Can you identify instances when you have engaged in selective listening, avoided the technical or difficult, or criticized the speaker's delivery or visual aids?

☐ Are you willing to listen?

☐ Do you make a habit of evaluating carefully and responding appropriately?

☐ Would you describe yourself as intellectually curious about matters relevant to your profession?

☐ Have you a method for recording the ideas that strike you as being important or potentially useful?

☐ Listening is a form of thinking. Do you use what people say as a stimulus for your own thoughts and creativity?

PART THREE
Develop Your Writing and Reading Skills

What is conceived well is expressed clearly
And words to say it will arise with ease.

Nicholas Boileau, French poet and literary critic

Writing effective letters, memos and reports, whether on paper or electronically, to customers or clients, local authorities or public bodies, is part and parcel of most jobs today.

Despite the advance in transmission technology, the actual business of writing an effective letter or memo comes back to your personal and professional skills as a writer. The first aim of Part Three is to help you to become really proficient on paper so that in this respect you are more than equal to the needs of your job.

Remember, however, that the art of communication is two way: speaking *and* listening, writing *and* reading. Moreover, these four basic personal skills overlap considerably. The qualities of a good reader are similar to those of a good listener, and both reading and listening contribute to your skills as a speaker and a writer. 'After three days without reading,' the Chinese say, 'talk becomes flavour-less.'

The second aim of Part Three, then, is to bring you up to speed as a reader. Not literally – I am no believer in speed reading – but in such a way that as a communicator you will have some ballast in the hold of your ship.

Nine Greatest Ideas for Clear Writing

Idea 45: Three elements of composition

Music has three common ingredients: melody, harmony and rhythm. On that analogy, all written compositions have three factors in common:

1 Structure and layout
2 Content
3 Style and tone

Structure and layout

Most of us are taught at school how to lay out a letter and structure it into paragraphs. Report writing is now also taught in the context of project work. But it is often the case that beginners overestimate the importance of structure or layout in writing. Usually if you are clear and say what you are doing, you can get away with almost anything. Conventions are important, but they are relatively easy to learn and certainly are not the main aspect of writing.

Content

Obviously I cannot advise you about *content* – what you are writing is all about – nor can any textbook on writing. I can help you to cook and present the dish, but the ingredients are yours alone. How the content of your written communication ultimately fares, however, will depend on its intrinsic merits or value in that strange marketplace where truth is bought and sold.

Style and tone

In theory it is possible to separate *content* from *form* – the structure and layout plus style and tone – but in practice it is difficult to do so. Therefore you shouldn't think of style and tone as an optional extra, like pink icing on a fruit cake, but as a critical factor in communicating effectively to others. To most intents and purposes, 'the medium is part of the message'.

> *'Have something to say and say it or write it as clearly as you can.'*

Idea 46: Say it as clearly as you can

If any man wishes to write in a clear style, let him first be clear in his thoughts.

Johann Wolfgang von Goethe, German writer

As early as the seventeenth century, the first historian of the Royal Society, Thomas Sprat, mentioned the Society's rejection of the 'amplifications, digressions and swellings of style' seen in contemporary writings, in favour of a 'close, natural and naked way of speaking'.

As Goethe suggests, if you are clear in your mind about what you want to say, the style of your writing will tend to reflect that clarity. Conversely, if your mind is muddled, so will be your style.

One test for clarity is to read aloud what you have just written. If it *sounds* sloppy, inconclusive, blurred, confused, doubtful, foggy, fuzzy, muddled, obscure, unintelligible or vague, then go back to the drawing board and try again!

When you do your next draft you will usually find that your writing gets a lot clearer, and consequently what you write begins to sound much more intelligible.

In fact, that's part of the fun of writing. 'Thinking is the activity I love best,' said science fiction author Isaac Asimov, 'and writing is simply thinking through my fingers.' Many centuries before St Augustine of Hypo had said much the same: 'I write as I progress, and I progress as I write.' The way to become clearer is to keep writing until what you write starts to look and sound clear.

> *'Every art requires the whole person.'*

Idea 47: On keeping it simple

Better one living word than a hundred dead ones.

German proverb

When you write you should think of yourself as talking directly to the person you are writing to. That is relatively easy if you are writing a love letter, but much more difficult if you are writing to people you don't know personally. Nevertheless, it can be done.

Once you start to see writing as a branch of speaking and not as a separate discipline, you can apply the same principles. Anyone who wishes to become a good writer should endeavour to be direct, simple, brief, vigorous and lucid.

This general principle may be translated into practical rules in the domain of vocabulary, as follows:

◆ Prefer the familiar word to the far-fetched.
◆ Prefer the concrete word to the abstract.
◆ Prefer the single word to the circumlocution.
◆ Prefer the short word to the long.
◆ Prefer the Saxon word to the Latin.

These rules are given roughly in order of merit: the last is also the least. Sometimes only a longish Latin-based word will do the job: the key word of this book, *communication*, is one good example, and *organization* is another.

The reason for following these principles is that you can be reasonably confident that all your readers or hearers will understand what you mean.

You can, of course, introduce a word that is on the edges of or outside the vocabulary of normal people; not to do so would be to deny to yourself and others the riches of the English language. But the principle is to remember if you do so always to indicate briefly what it means. That saves your reader the time and trouble of looking the word up in a dictionary when you want them to be attending to what you are saying.

> *'By writing we learn to write.'*

Idea 48: Do a first draft

The golden rule in all writing is to get something down on paper or up on screen and then play about with it. An important business letter deserves that kind of careful treatment. Here are seven factors to consider in revising your draft:

Objective	The objective or message of the letter should be clear. What response you expect or would like from the reader – if any – should also be clearly expressed.
Order	You may want to revise the order of your points or paragraphs within the broad parameters of *beginning*, *middle* and *end*.
Style	Check the lengths of your paragraphs and sentences. Try reading the letter out loud. Take out unintended repetitions. Avoid jargon.
Word selection	Cut out obscure words and clichés, as well as adverbial verbiage such as 'by and large', 'on the whole' or 'all things being equal'.
Tone	Carry out a tone check on the letter. Is it set in the right musical key? Does the tone accurately reflect your feelings? If necessary, tone down, or tone up.
Grammar/ spelling	Check the grammar and punctuation. Avoid any spelling mistakes if possible: they may create amusement if not annoyance in the reader, distracting them from your message. Computer spell check and grammar tools can easily help you do this if you are writing electronically. An up-to-date dictionary is helpful if you are using pen and paper.
Layout	Does the layout look attractive? Does it sell to the eye? Word-processing technology can help you to format or professionally lay out a letter using guidance or a template. Make use of these tools.

Remember to check through and correct the final draft. Then choose the appropriate form of greeting and signature. Ensure that you have attached the relevant enclosures and that you have kept a copy for your file.

'All writing is rewriting.'

Idea 49: How to get the tone right

Courteous asking breaks down even city walls.

Ukrainian proverb

The *Oxford English Dictionary* defines tone as 'a particular quality, pitch, modulation, or inflection of the voice expressing . . . affirmation, interrogation, hesitation, decision, or some feeling or emotion'. Business letters are more likely to be effective if they are written in a tone of courtesy. Watch out for the negative viruses that can so easily infect the tone of your letters.

Some negative elements of tone

Curtness	The virus of inordinate brevity communicates unconcern for your reader.
Sarcasm	Most people dislike being on the receiving end of this so-called form of wit, which ridicules by saying the opposite of what you mean.
Peevishness	Includes such whining remarks as 'You ought to know better.'
Anger	The roar of anger, even if it is under your breath, usually provokes an answering roar.
Suspicion	Often takes the form of being suspicious or even cynical about motives.
Insult	Intentional insults are rare, but unintentional ones are not uncommon – especially in replies to applications for jobs.
Accusation	It is obviously difficult to point an accusing finger and maintain courtesy.
Talking down	'In an establishment as large as ours, Miss Smith . . .' The didactic or instructional tone grates in letters, and any teaching has to be done with a light touch.

(Continued)

Presumptuousness	Don't presume that someone will do something before they have made up their mind to do it or include this presumption in a letter, as it could offend. The line between confidence and presumption is a fine one.

Ask yourself
Will the reader hear what I say if the tone of my letter is shouting at them?

Idea 50: The effective letter

The wise read a letter backwards.

German proverb

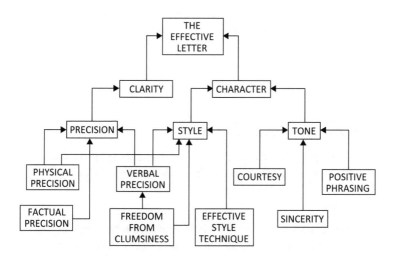

Idea 51: Keep it as brief as you can

Brevity or conciseness is especially important in business or purposeful writing. 'I think' is much better than 'In my opinion it is considered not an unjustifiable assumption that'.

George Bernard Shaw made the definitive comment here when he handed a letter to a friend by saying: 'I am sorry this letter is so long but I didn't have time to make it short.'

Case study: Winston Churchill

On 9 August 1940, Winston Churchill sent round a memo to his colleagues in the wartime coalition government of Britain. Here it is:

Brevity

To do our work we all have to read a mass of papers. Nearly all of them are far too long. This wastes time, while energy has to be spent on looking for essential points.

I ask my colleagues and their staff to see that their reports are shorter.

1. The aim should be reports which set out the main points in a series of short, crisp paragraphs.
2. If a report relies on detailed analysis of some complicated factors or on statistics, these should be set out in an appendix.
3. Often the occasion is best met by submitting not a full report, but a reminder consisting of headings only, which can be expounded orally if needed.
4. Let us have an end to such phrases as these: 'it is also important to bear in mind the following considerations . . . or consideration should be given to the possibility of carrying into effect . . .' Most

of these woolly phrases are mere padding, which can be left out altogether, or replaced by a single word. Let us not shrink from using the short expressive phrase, even if it is conversational.

Reports drawn up on the lines I propose may at first seem rough as compared with the flat surface of officialese jargon, but the saving in time will be great, while the discipline of setting out the real points concisely will prove an aid to clearer thinking.

Remind yourself
Use exactly as many words as are required to express something and no more.

Idea 52: How to write an effective report

A report is an official or formal statement, often made after an investigation and usually by a subordinate to a superior. Like Caesar's Gaul, a report falls into three parts.

Beginning

Your report should begin with an introduction, which sets out the essential background and crystallizes the aim and objectives of the report. The latter will already have been foreshadowed by the title. The format, like a book in miniature, should include the name of the author and the date of compilation.

Middle

The middle body of evidence, information, issues and discussions should be clearly and succinctly arranged in a simple order, signposted by chapters, major and minor side headings and numbered paragraphs.

End

The concluding section must leave the reader in no doubt as to the writer's conclusions and recommendations.

Points to remember

◆ Your key assumptions should be made manifest at the appropriate places; difficult or technical terms should always be defined.

◆ Illustrations, sharing the characteristics of a speaker's good visual aids, can save time and space in the main text, but complicated supporting data should appear as appendices at the end.

◆ The minimum requirements for style are not different from those needed for letters or any other forms of business writing.

◆ Above all, the report should achieve its stated objective with economy of words, especially where the written word is to be used in alliance with speech.

Ask yourself
What would I make of this report if I received it?

Idea 53: Checklist – How good is your report?

Structure and layout

☐ Is the title page complete and well laid out?

☐ Is the layout clear and easy to follow?

☐ Are any essential parts of the structure missing?

☐ Are the main parts of the structure in the most suitable order for this report?

☐ Do headings stand out?

☐ Is the numbering of paragraphs uniform?

☐ Are the appendices clear and helpful?

Content

☐ Is the summary or abstract (if included) confined to essentials and a fair statement?

☐ Does the introduction state clearly:

◆ The subject and the purpose of the report?

◆ The date of the investigation?

◆ By whom the report was written?

◆ For whom the report was written?

◆ The scope of the report?

☐ Does the main part of the report contain all the necessary facts and no unnecessary information?

☐ Is the order of the main part of the report right?

☐ Is the problem clearly stated?

- ☐ Does detail obscure the main issue?
- ☐ Are the sources of facts clear?
- ☐ Do conclusions follow logically from the facts and their interpretation?
- ☐ Are possible solutions abandoned without reason?
- ☐ Are terms, abbreviations and symbols used, suitable and consistent?
- ☐ Are there any statements whose meaning is not quite clear?
- ☐ Are facts, figures and calculations accurate?

General

- ☐ Is the report objective?
- ☐ Can the report's recommendations be criticized?
- ☐ Is the report efficient and businesslike and likely to create a good impression?
- ☐ Could a non-technical person directly or indirectly concerned with the report understand it?
- ☐ Could anyone reasonably take offence at anything in the report?
- ☐ Is the report positive and constructive?
- ☐ Does it make clear what decision, if any, is required and by whom?

Six Greatest Ideas for the Art of Reading

Idea 54: The effective reader

Reading makes a full man; conference a ready man; and writing an exact man.

Francis Bacon, English philosopher and writer

'It is the good reader that makes the good book,' said the American writer and philosopher Ralph Waldo Emerson. But what makes a good reader?

Reading is the fourth of the core skills of communication. Perhaps more than listening it is the forgotten or neglected one. Few books on communication give it the space it deserves.

One difficulty is that the English language doesn't have separate terms equivalent to *hearing* and *listening* for the written or printed word, and so *reading* covers them both. Reading can be merely taking in or comprehending what is on paper or screen.

However, good reading is listening in action again, giving time and thoughtful attention to what you are reading and remaining alive to all the possibilities it suggests. In other words, you need to be open and receptive to what the writer has to say. To have an open mind when you are young is easy; to keep it open as you grow older is an art.

The four skills – speaking, listening, writing and reading – are not separate entities: they interact with and enrich each other. It's a package deal. If you never read, for example, if nothing less it will affect your vocabulary and hence your ability to speak, listen or write.

> *'The mind does not grow old.'*

Idea 55: Some reading challenges

The problems facing the reader who wants a good, digestible meal are largely created by the poor culinary skills of the writer. They include:

- ◆ Poor structure
- ◆ Unattractive appearance and layout
- ◆ Turgid and repetitive style
- ◆ Unnecessary length
- ◆ Lack of examples or illustrations
- ◆ Obscure diagrams
- ◆ Dense or opaque thought processes
- ◆ Too much information
- ◆ Too little information
- ◆ Unpalatable tone

A good reader, in parallel with a good listener, will not be totally fazed by the surface phenomena, especially if he or she feels that gold lies beneath it. Like a gold prospector you may come away with some gold dust or even a nugget, even though the latter may, on later examination, turn out to be 'fool's gold'.

When you encounter the kind of difficulties listed above, don't give up on reading if you suspect there is some truth struggling to get out. As a bonus, take it as an object lesson in how not to write for others.

In reading books you have to know when to cut your losses and call it a day. Books are like houses: knock three times and if no answer comes from inside, go away and read another book.

Idea 56: Identify your reading priorities

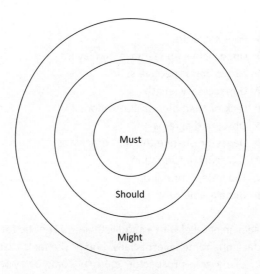

Must

Should

Might

Reading priorities

To help you clarify your reading requirement, go to the core of your job: what are you paid to do?

- ◆ What *must* you read?
- ◆ What *should* you read?
- ◆ What *might* you read?

A consultant neurologist, for example, *must* read certain journals in order to keep up to date. He or she *should* read about developments in related fields, such as the care of long-term patients with spinal injuries. The *might* category covers a wide range of possibilities, but in this instance it could include reading a book on developments in healthcare in Europe or the US.

Your list will, no doubt, be somewhat similar. Each day on your desk there will be letters, proposals, reports and memos that you *must* read, along with material that falls into the *should* and *might* categories.

Now look again at your job. Arguably, you are paid both to do your job and to improve your job. Does your reading requirement reflect that second dimension?

If I may point the question, what have you read in the last six months that has led you to *improve* your existing job as opposed to doing what you were hired to do?

There is also a third dimension. Put briefly, no organization is going to guarantee you the same job for life. We are all on short-term contracts of one kind or another. As well as fulfilling today's role you ought to be preparing for tomorrow's job, one that you may be able only dimly to discern.

In other words, with or without the help of your organization or employer, you need to be developing your future capability as well as your present competence. And reading books, stores of information and ideas, is an important element in that process of self-education or self-development.

Most books, of course, are read for entertainment or amusement. No harm in that. What better way to give your mind a holiday?

Idea 57: Develop the skill of scanning

'What, have you not read it through?' the Scottish author James Boswell once asked.

'No, Sir,' replied his friend Dr Johnson. 'Do you read books through?'

Life presents us with too much information, so we have to learn to be selective. Otherwise our mind would drown in a torrent of words.

Scanning involves the action of quickly glancing down the body of a text so that the mind can rapidly take in the gist of what is written.

The word 'scan' comes from the Latin *scandere* meaning 'to climb or leap', so imagine yourself jumping quickly from stepping stone to stepping stone without getting your feet wet in the text.

It should be a wide, sweeping, methodical search, quick but not hasty. *Festine lente,* 'make haste slowly'. Scanning should also be an intensive examination, not a superficial one. It takes time, but it will save you time as well.

This leaping from point to point gives you an overall picture. It may lead you to scrutinize much more carefully parts of the written text.

'Scrutiny' is another word we took from Latin; it derives from the word *scrutinium* meaning 'trash or rubbish'. So the original scrutiny took place on the rubbish dumps of ancient Rome as the poor sorted out usable rags. The word stresses close attention to minute detail. Your thoughtful attention – the essence of good reading as of good listening – has now moved from wide angle to narrow focus.

To read a book for the first time is to make the acquaintance of a new friend; to read it a second time is to meet an old one.

Chinese saying

Idea 58: Guidelines for effective scanning

Some books are to be read only in parts; others to be read but not curiously; and some few to be read wholly, and with diligence and attention.

Francis Bacon, English philosopher and writer

1. Prepare by previewing the *content* of the piece that interests you – study the title, subheadings, illustrations and the writer's aims in writing.
2. Look at the writer's pattern – the structure plan or *method* that he or she has adopted – the table of contents, rough lengths of chapters, appendices and notes.
3. Sample one or two paragraphs to test the writing: density of thought, tone, intelligibility, the 'ring of truth'.
4. Scan – if you're still interested – the whole or selected parts, looking more closely for the necklace thread of the argument or theme: key paragraphs, sentences or words.
5. Develop your actual reading speed with long, rhythmic eye sweeps, both horizontal and vertical.
6. Examine more closely the parts or passages that especially interest you, rereading where necessary.

Idea 59: Reading in depth

A good book is the lifeblood of a master-spirit, embalmed and treasured up for a life beyond life.

John Milton, English poet

Some articles, reports or books merit both careful reading and reflective thinking. They are literally food for thought.

 Ask yourself

- ◆ Am I clear about my purpose in reading any piece of writing with this depth of interest and attention?
- ◆ Have I some definite questions in mind that I am seeking to answer?
- ◆ Are they the right questions?
- ◆ Do I continually ask myself questions as I read to stay focused on the subject?
- ◆ Do I read to glean the main ideas? Can I identify the main idea in each chapter, and the contributing ideas in each section and each paragraph?
- ◆ Do I critically test the evidence, explanations, examples and other detail offered as grounds for the writer's case?
- ◆ Do I have suitable methods of making notes or recording what I learn or can use?
- ◆ Do I match or compare the writer's experience with my own? If so, does my experience lend weight to the writer's conclusions?
- ◆ Is any of it worth reading again (now or later on)?
- ◆ Should I discuss the material with anyone? (Who? Why? When? How? What?)

'Reading is to the mind what exercise is to the body.'

Follow-up test

Clear writing

- [ ] Do you always make clarity your principal concern in anything you write?
- [ ] Would you agree that being clear starts in your mind and then flows through your fingers onto the page or computer screen?
- [ ] In choosing words, do you cut out any unnecessary jargon and express yourself in plain English?
- [ ] In revising a draft, do you pay special attention to getting the tone just right?
- [ ] Do you consistently aim for conciseness in all that you write?
- [ ] Are the reports you write clearly divided into three parts: beginning, middle and end? Does each part deliver on its proper functions?

The art of reading

- [ ] When you read, do you do so with an open and receptive mind?
- [ ] Are you too easily deterred by the barriers unconsciously erected by an incompetent writer?
- [ ] Do you have a clear idea of your reading priorities?
- [ ] There is too much information and therefore one has to be selective. How good are you at scanning reports, memos, letters and books?
- [ ] Can you think of three books that have really gripped your attention, so that you have devoured, inwardly digested and made their contents your own?

PART FOUR
The Manager as Communicator

Countless studies of what managers actually do daily highlights the centrality of communication. The business of being on the telephone, emailing, dealing with correspondence, attending meetings, interviewing, giving presentations is not interruptions or distractions from their work – it *is* their work.

Part Four focuses on three 'set pieces' of communication in the life of a busy manager: giving presentations, taking part in and chairing meetings, and conducting interviews.

With regard to interviews, as this isn't a textbook I have happily resisted the temptation to cover all the different types of interviews. Rather, I have focused mainly on the appraisal interview, because I think it poses to both interviewer and interviewee the greatest of all communication challenges: giving and receiving criticism. To become a great leader you have to master that double-sided art.

Ten Greatest Ideas for Giving Presentations

Idea 60: Practical presentation skills

The word *presentation* has almost taken over from *public speaking* as a general term. Plenty of occasions arise, such as:

◆ Making a marketing or sales proposal.
◆ Launching a new product or service.
◆ Speaking at a seminar or conference.
◆ Running a training session.
◆ Presenting your business plan.

Please add two other examples from your own field. Try to think ahead. If your career plans work out, what sort of occasions for speaking in public will arise?

You can see at once the importance of presentational skills for you. Quite apart from the impact they may have on your business in terms of bottom-line results, presentations are also high-profile events for you personally. To some extent you will be on trial and you will be judged. In some contexts your career or progress may even depend on your performances.

Therefore your aim should be to develop your presentational skills, so that you can present with confidence and effect on all the occasions that are likely to arise. Those skills include the abilities to:

◆ Profile the occasion, audience and location.
◆ Plan and write the presentation.
◆ Use visual aids (if appropriate).
◆ Prepare your talk.
◆ Rehearse (with others if necessary).
◆ Deliver on the day.

All of these are important, for each contributes to your overall effectiveness as a presenter. You may not be able to control or manage some of the factors – locations, for example – but you should ensure that everything that can be done to promote success has been done. You will then approach the day with your natural apprehension balanced by a growing confidence and expectation of success.

Idea 61: Profile the occasion

When planning a presentation, there is one thing you should do before anything else: profile the occasion, audience and location.

You should ask yourself the following questions.

The occasion

- ◆ What kind is it?
- ◆ What are its aims?
- ◆ What time is allowed?
- ◆ What else is happening?

The audience

- ◆ Do they know anything about me?
- ◆ Do I know its size?
- ◆ What do they expect?
- ◆ Why are they there?
- ◆ What is their knowledge level?
- ◆ Do I know any of them personally/professionally?
- ◆ Do I expect friendliness, indifference or hostility?
- ◆ Will they be able to use what they hear?

The location

- ◆ Do I know the room size, seating arrangements, layout/set-up and acoustics?

◆ Do I know the technical arrangements for use of micro-
phones, audio-visuals, lighting and whether assistance is
available (and have I notified my requirements in
advance)?

◆ Do I know who will control room temperature, lighting
and moving people in and out?

Occasion, audience and location are interactive. I have known an
otherwise successful conference virtually ruined by the slowness of
service and very low quality of food in the hotel (not booked by me,
I might add!).

> *'Time spent on reconnaissance is seldom wasted.'*

Idea 62: Checklist – occasion, audience, location

The occasion

☐ Do you know the aim or objective of the presentation?
☐ Are you clear what kind of occasion it is?
☐ Is there sufficient time for the presentation?
☐ Has time been allowed for discussion?
☐ Do you know who will chair the session and introduce you?
☐ Do they have biographical information about you?
☐ Have you grasped the context of your presentation, what is happening before and after?

The audience

☐ Do you know how many people there will be?
☐ Can you assess their motivation for being there?
☐ Have you an accurate idea of their expectations?
  Is the knowledge level of the audience in relation to your subject:
☐ High?
☐ Mixed?
☐ Low?
☐ Do you know any of them personally or professionally?
  All in all, do you expect them to be:
☐ Unusually friendly?
☐ Indifferent?

☐ Hostile?
☐ Will they be able to use what they hear?

_____

_____

The location
_____

Have you a clear picture in your mind of the following:
☐ Room size?
☐ Seating arrangements?
☐ Platform/lectern?
☐ Acoustics?
☐ Public address equipment?
☐ Audio-visual equipment?
☐ Technical assistance?
☐ Room temperature?
☐ Lighting controls?
☐ Refreshments?

Idea 63: Planning and writing your presentation

Usually it is possible to define your aim in terms of the results that should follow from a presentation. These may fall into broad areas, such as change, commitment, action or understanding. It is then necessary, if possible, to break them down to more specific objectives by asking 'What change?', 'Commitment to what?' or 'Understanding what in particular?'

Having written down your objective or objectives, focused at the right level of specificity for the expected audience, your next job is to sketch out a framework or skeleton of your presentation. Reduced to its most simple form it should have a *beginning*, *middle* and *end*.

Phase	Notes
Beginning	Introduction by chair.
	Your introductory remarks.
	State your objective(s) and give some reasons why they are relevant to the audience.
	Signpost the main outlines of the presentation.
Middle	Break the complex whole of the presentation down into manageable parts, just as an author divides a book into chapters. Three, four, five or six sections, usually no more.
	Make sure that you illustrate the main points by examples or support them by evidence.
	A half-time summary is often a good idea, especially if it is a longish and complicated presentation.
	Put a time estimate against each of these parts or sections and double check that most time goes on the top priorities.
End	A summary is often a good way to initiate the last phase.
	Don't leave your conclusions to chance. Refer back to your objective and prepare your final remarks with that in mind.

At all costs avoid the not uncommon sequence of *beginning, muddle* and *no end*!

Idea 64: Using visual aids

Why use visual aids? Because we take in much of our information, more than 50 per cent, through the gateway of our eyes. Therefore there is always a strong case for using visual aids, especially if your presentation is primarily about conveying information.

Some general tips for using visual aids

1. Use a series of pictures to structure your presentation for you and allow you to look at the audience while developing each point. Look at the audience more than the pictures on the screen.
2. Present only essential information on each picture.
3. Restrict the content to about 25 words or the equivalent in figures.
4. Make sure that any slides or frames are clearly numbered in the correct sequence and are the right way up. Any confusion will damage your professional image.
5. Use pictures, drawings and colour for interest.
6. Don't leave any one visual aid on for too long.
7. Above all, do not overload your presentation with too many slides or pictures. Less is more.
8. If you're using high-tech equipment then make sure you have someone on hand who can help with any technical hitches; this includes everything from locating power points to dealing with a crashed computer

> 'A picture is worth a thousand words.'

Idea 65: Rehearse with the others involved

Presentations are often given by two or three people working as a team. That calls for teamwork and *that* calls for a practice session or rehearsal. In fact you may need more than one rehearsal before an important presentation.

Remember, however, that unless you are careful you can over-rehearse, which kills spontaneity. A good orchestra will rehearse several times but always leave something in reserve. There has to be some magic on the night of the actual performance.

The mutual constructive criticism that follows each run-through will lead to improvements. Above all, as a team you can approach the event with full confidence in each other and in the clarity of the message you wish to put across.

This practice session allows you to tune up your own instrument, going through your part and hearing the sound of your voice in that particular room. It promotes a smooth and graceful coordination of effort among the team.

Finally, it enables you to check out all the equipment and visual aids. Are they legible from the back row or far corner of the room, for instance?

Idea 66: How best to deliver your presentation on the day

If you have done your homework you shouldn't encounter any big surprises when you come to give your presentation. There may, however, be some changes on the day that you haven't anticipated and in that case you must make a judgement about making alterations to the content or methods of your presentation.

Having done that, you and the audience are ready to go on the journey together. Now everything depends on your delivery skills.

Delivering your presentation

Beginning	If the chairman's introduction needs to be corrected, do it courteously and with thanks.
	Capture your audience. Explain the background and objectives for the presentation in as concise, clear and vital a way as possible, giving your audience time to tune into your voice and accustom themselves to you as a person.
	Tell them what you intend to do – and why.
Middle	'Grace, pace and space' – the hallmarks of a good motor car – should characterize your presentation.
	Keep it moving as you cover your prepared points with professional ease.
	Let the audience know in advance if you want them to ask clarifying questions as you talk or to save them until after you have finished.
	Try to sweep the whole audience with your eyes as you speak, so that everyone feels included.
	Remember to vary the tone of your voice and not to speak too fast or too low.
	Look pleasant – people like looking at someone who appears to be enjoying themselves.

(Continued)

End	Signal to your audience when you are entering the end phase.
	Don't introduce new ideas or information, but consolidate what you have done.
	End on a high note if you can: a short, strong conclusion.
	Always prepare carefully and learn your last two or three sentences.
Questions/ discussion	Repeat any questions that may be inaudible to parts of the audience.
	Try not to be long-winded in answering them.
	Promote discussion by asking a few questions of your own.
	Make sure that all the lights are on in this phase. Always be courteous and express appreciation.
	Disentangle multipart questions and answer each part separately.
Conclusion	Avoid the session petering out by further summarizing the discussion and reinforcing any action points.
	Close with some words of thanks.

Idea 67: How to calm your nerves

The mere fact of having to take part in a presentation is enough to set the alarm bells ringing in an inexperienced manager's mind. No wonder that he or she is often plagued by nerves before such public exposure.

Ask yourself
Do I ever feel self-conscious if I have to stand up and speak to a group, even if I know them quite well?

Do I experience difficulty in finding the right words to express myself clearly?

Do I get unpleasant symptoms, such as palpitations, feeling sick, a dry mouth, sweaty palms or breathlessness?

Does my mind ever go completely blank before I stand up to speak?

Do I fear it might and that I will then forget what I was going to say and make a fool of myself?

How can you learn to cope with your nerves? The first step is to realize that nerves are normal, so don't be alarmed by them.

Some degree of nervous tension before a presentation is actually a good thing. It gets the adrenalin flowing and prepares your mind and body for a superlative performance. Some simple relaxation exercises, like deep breathing, can help to keep these pre-event nerves in a manageable state.

Why does nervousness happen? Your body cannot distinguish too well between different kinds of danger. Prompted by your mind, it interprets a public presentation as a danger situation, which arouses anxiety, if not fear.

Why should it do this? Probably because being watched by a large number of people reminds our primitive selves of being potential victims under observation from hungry predators or enemies lying in wait in an ambush. Our body changes prepare us for fight or flight. If you are wounded in a fight, for example, it's better not to have food in your stomach. So it is natural to feel or be sick on the threshold of perceived danger situations.

You can see that *perception* plays a large part in keeping these natural physical reactions within manageable proportions.

The most important step is therefore to change your perception of your audience. No actor could go on stage every night if he or she perceived the audience to be hostile. There are occasionally hostile audiences, but on the whole we go to the theatre in a positive frame of mind, wanting to be entertained or enlightened and willing the cast to succeed. Half the battle is to persuade yourself that the audience is on your side, either already or potentially so. Why else would they be there?

> *'There are no bad audiences, only bad speakers.'*

Idea 68: Six tips to build your confidence

1. *Breathe deeply.*
   Breathe well down into your lungs. This enables your diaphragm to control the release of breath from your lungs as you utter each word.

2. *Manage your hands.*
   If your hands seem to 'get in your way', clasp them loosely in front of you or place them behind your back. Train yourself to forget them.

3. *Look at your audience.*
   Look at your audience all the time you are speaking and embrace them all in your glance. Try to forget yourself in the urge to communicate.

4. *Move well.*
   Let your movements be deliberate and unhurried. In a big hall, make your gestures a little larger than life. Gestures spring spontaneously from the words that are on your lips, so don't try to rehearse them – it will look stilted. When speaking on a formal occasion you can move about if you wish, but the most comfortable anchor stance is to have your feet placed slightly apart and the weight of the body thrown slightly forward onto the balls of the feet. There is then no fidgeting or unnecessary movement.

5. *Talk slowly.*
   Do not let your rate of utterance exceed your rate of thought. Only in this way can you avoid the danger of 'stumbling' over your words. In fact, do not think of *words* now – think only of ideas and mind pictures.

6.   *Compose yourself and relax.*
     Always allow yourself some minutes to clear your mind
     of the matters that have been occupying it before
     the presentation. If you relax, your audience will do the
     same.

Idea 69: Speaking without notes

If I am to speak for ten minutes, I need a week of preparation; if fifteen minutes, three days; if half-an-hour, two days; if an hour, I am ready now.

US President Woodrow Wilson

Why not speak without notes? If you are a professional speaker, you should always do so. It is not such a difficult art to master as you may think. Actors, comedians and concert musicians do not refer to notes, so why should you? The practice of doing so leaves you free to look at your audience and to think on your feet. It does take more time in preparation, but it is invariably worth it.

By 'learning the part' I don't mean committing a fully written-out script to memory, as the actor or comedian or musician does before going on stage. You have to memorize the plan – the structure of skeleton of your presentation – together with any facts, quotations, stories or examples.

The test is that you must be confident that you can give the presentation without recourse to notes. Your short-term memory is probably much more trustworthy than you imagine. Does it matter if you get the odd word or phrase wrong?

In between the extremes of reading out a prepared script and talking without notes there are several other options. If it is a 'one-off' presentation and if you lack confidence to abandon your notes altogether, you could use your slides or flipchart sheets as notes.

Keep a copy of your presentation notes on you or near you so that you can glance at them once you're on stage. Never be afraid to fish it out and look at it during your presentation if you momentarily lose your bearings.

Twelve Greatest Ideas for Leading Effective Meetings

Idea 70: Why meetings matter

If people are of one heart, even the yellow earth can become gold.

Chinese proverb

Meetings proliferate but they have acquired a bad name for ineffectiveness, time wasting and sheer lack of fun. As the witches said in Shakespeare's *Macbeth*:

When shall we three meet again
In thunder, lightning, or in rain?

Managers will certainly meet in better conditions than those witches on their blasted heath, but they definitely know that they will be meeting again – and again!

Meeting is a very general word that encompasses any situation in which two or more people come together by accident or design, in an encounter that may be momentary or prolonged. Almost all of them involve some form of communication. But the meetings that concern us here are those that involve a group of people who meet for discussion with a purpose. How do you lead or manage that discussion effectively?

Meetings are essential and, as we all know, they can be enjoyable as well as productive. It all depends on the quality of the discussion. Without good discussion there will be no clarity; without clarity there will be no sound agreement; and without a basis of agreement there will certainly be no effective action.

That is why it is important for you to master the art of leading effective meetings.

Idea 71: Five essentials for effective discussion

To some people discussion suggests a rambling or freewheeling conversation in which people express their views or sentiments to each other – just the sort of thing to be banned from efficient, tightly controlled and brisk meetings!

But rightly understood, discussion lies at the core of all purposeful meetings. It should be differentiated from conversation on the one hand and formal debate on the other. It ought to be limited to a given theme. More often than not, discussion is a way of reaching conclusions or determining a course of action.

The actual word 'discussion' comes from a Latin root, *discutere*, which originally means 'to shake apart'. Possibilities are sifted or shaken apart. Their pros and cons are considered.

For this work to be done effectively, five ingredients need to be present:

1. *Planning* in advance is essential to successful discussion. It is futile to rely on spontaneous combustion to develop profitable talk. The initiative for this planning may be taken by a designated leader, but it is better when at least some members of the group can work on it together.

2. *Informality* is desirable to encourage the fullest possible participation, although the size of the group or audience and the seating arrangements in the meeting place impose some limits. Organized informality best describes this objective.

3. *Participation* is an essential ingredient of good discussion, for this method assumes that each individual may

have something of value to contribute and that the cooperative pooling of all available information is the best way to find the right solution.

In small groups the optimum size, research shows, is seven, and everyone who wishes to may speak; in a large public discussion only a few can have the floor, but it should be emphasized that active listening is participation.

4. *Purpose* is essential in good discussion. Merely pleasant or socially useful talk that skips from one topic to another is not discussion as conceived here.

5. *Leadership* in some form is necessary for a successful discussion. In public meetings, a leader or chairperson is necessary. In small groups, whose members know each other, the functions of leadership may sometimes be shared by various individuals.

Idea 72: Eight attributes of a good discussion leader

To lead a group discussion and also contribute to the discussion from time to time yourself, you will need to develop a set of leadership characteristics:

1. Clear and rapid thinking.
2. Attentive listening.
3. The ability to express yourself clearly and succinctly.
4. Being ready to clarify badly expressed views.
5. The ability to be impartial and impersonal.
6. Being a preventer of inappropriate interruptions.
7. Patience, tolerance and kindness.
8. The ability to be friendly but brisk and businesslike.

Idea 73: Keeping the discussion on course

As chairperson you should remember to begin the meeting by saying what its purpose is and why it is necessary. Don't assume that everyone knows. You may also want to check that the participants are comfortable with the agenda, so that *your* plan for the meeting now becomes *our* plan for it. In a pleasant but firm way, show that you have taken charge.

If a long-winded person still challenges you for the right of way, by continuing to talk over others or by interrupting again, then you will have to show some steel until they get the message. Never lose control.

Heading off potential or actual irrelevancies is also a vital part of controlling a meeting. Sometimes a 'red herring' looks more tasty than the 'bread-and-butter' items on the agenda. However, where the object of a meeting is creative thinking, as in brainstorming sessions, it may sometimes be worth pursuing red herrings, for the apparently irrelevant may disguise the germ of a new idea.

Once work has started on the agenda you will have to exercise the function of *controlling*, which should be done with intelligence and sensitivity. What would you do about an overtalkative person? It is essential to stop them, but it has to be done tactfully as well as firmly: 'Thank you, Michael, I think we have got the drift of your argument. Susan, you haven't said anything yet. Do you agree with Michael or not?'

Experienced colleagues at a discussion meeting will seldom require you to exercise the *gatekeeping* function of 'opening the door' for someone to make a contribution. More often than not, your energies will be deployed in shutting the door!

Idea 74: Five types of meeting

You will encounter and take part in five main types of meetings at work. It is useful to bear them in mind, because it helps you to prepare for them in advance.

1. *A briefing meeting.*

   A briefing meeting is called by the manager to direct or instruct their team members to undertake a particular task or to lay down policy governing future conduct. It is characterized by:

   ◆ Giving instructions and information.

   ◆ Clearing up misunderstandings.

   ◆ Integrating ideas and views where appropriate.

2. *An advisory meeting.*

   An advisory meeting is called essentially for the exchange of information. It is not a decision-making meeting as such. It is characterized by:

   ◆ Seeking advice about a problem.

   ◆ Informing others about ideas.

   ◆ Listening to views.

3. *A council meeting.*

   A council meeting is held between people of equal standing who have some professional knowledge or skill to contribute. It is characterized by:

   ◆ Decisions being made by consensus.

   ◆ Accountability lying with the group.

   ◆ Resolving differences by talking through them.

4. *A committee meeting.*

   A committee meeting is one in which representatives from various groups or interests meet on a roughly equal footing to make decisions on matters of common concern. It is characterized by:

◆ A sense of authority.
◆ Differences ultimately being resolved by voting.
◆ Compromises being common.

5. *A negotiating meeting.*

A negotiating meeting is also one in which representatives of different interests meet, but decisions are made more on a bargaining basis than by voting. It is characterized by:

◆ Decisions being taken on a *quid pro quo* basis.
◆ Each side having different but overlapping aims.
◆ Each side seeking to achieve the best terms for itself.

'Nothing is impossible until it is sent to a committee.'

Idea 75: How to have productive meetings

Becoming more cost-conscious about meetings will help you to be economical with time. Check if any given meeting is really necessary and ensure that people don't waste their time attending meetings if their presence is not required. Time spent on planning the meeting will repay itself tenfold. Work out the agenda carefully, allotting time for each item.

Ask yourself
Is this meeting really necessary?

Careful preparation is the secret of productive meetings. First and foremost, it is essential that the chairperson be clear about the objective or objectives of the proposed meeting. A useful way of double checking is to ask yourself: 'Where should we all be at the end of this meeting?'

The *agenda* is the key factor in preparation. It shouldn't be just a list of headings to jog your memory during a meeting. Draw it up with thought, indicating whether an item is for discussion or decision.

Briefly describe the matter or subject. 'Mounting costs', for example, is too brief and vague. 'Mounting costs: to discuss the report on energy conservation in the factory and make decisions on the first and third recommendations on p. 16' is much more definite. It gives people the opportunity to think about the matter beforehand.

Ensure that everyone receives the agenda and relevant papers – in this case the 'Energy Conservation Report' – at least five clear days before the meeting.

Idea 76: Four practical ways to prepare

1. *Determine the purpose of the meeting.*
   Consider possible aims, such as:
   - ◆ To engage in joint consultation.
   - ◆ To develop support for action.
   - ◆ To resolve unsolved problems.
2. *Explore the subject.*
   - ◆ Collect/research facts and information.
   - ◆ Identify main topics to be discussed.
   - ◆ Consider probable differences in viewpoint.
3. *Outline the discussion.*
   - ◆ Set the end aim or objective.
   - ◆ Consider intermediate objectives.
   - ◆ Frame questions to develop discussion.
   - ◆ Plan the introduction especially and include the main topics for discussion.
   - ◆ Prepare a timetable for the meeting.
4. *Have everything ready.*
   - ◆ Issue invitations and information in good time.
   - ◆ Arrange accommodation.
   - ◆ Prepare necessary materials, include aids such as flipcharts or digital presentations.

Remember that people take in information more readily through their eyes than their ears. Visual aids should therefore play a part in your meetings more often than not; if they are clear, simple and vivid they can save you time.

If you go into a meeting clear about the objectives, having thought about the subject in advance and with everything ready, it is already most likely that your meeting will be effective.

Ask yourself

Out of the four practical steps above, which is my *strongest* and which is my *weakest*?

Idea 77: Checklist – Are you ready for take-off?

- ☐ Are you clear about the purpose of this planned discussion?
- ☐ Do the other participants know that purpose?
- ☐ If not, do you plan to communicate it to them before the meeting?
- ☐ Have you circulated any necessary information well before the meeting?
- ☐ Have you identified the main topics to be discussed? Is each objective clear?
- ☐ Have you framed some questions to stimulate discussion?
- ☐ Have you prepared a timetable for the meeting?
- ☐ Is the accommodation and seating plan arranged?
- ☐ Are all necessary materials ready, including visual aids and flipcharts?

Idea 78: Six rules for chairing a meeting

Making meetings effective

	1. Start on time
Aim	**2. Outline the purpose clearly**
	State the problems/situation/reason for the meeting
	Define constraints and limitations
	Establish the task(s) of the meeting
Guide	**3. Ensure effective discussion**
	Introduce the topic(s) for discussion
	Draw out opinions, viewpoints and experiences
	Develop group interest and involvement
	Keep the discussion within staged task(s)
Crystallize	**4. Establish conclusions**
	Recognize degrees of feeling and changes of opinion
	Summarize points of agreement and disagreement
	State intermediate conclusions as they are reached
	Check understanding and acceptance
Act	**5. Gain acceptance and commitment**
	Summarize and state conclusion(s) clearly
	Gain commitment to the action plan
	State responsibility for action
	Make sure that everybody understands
	6. End on time

Idea 79: The art of summarizing

A summary is a useful tool. It is a bare outline of the main points without details, an abridged or condensed statement of the issues at stake or what has been agreed so far.

It is in fact, if you think about it, a rare gift to be able to condense into as few words as possible an extended train or complex web of thought. It is a valuable tool to have in your toolkit.

Don't always leave your attempt at a summary to the end. One important way of guiding a discussion is to *summarize* progress so far, so that the remaining agenda or issues stand out clearly. Thus a summary given during a meeting – rather than in conclusion – can act as a trumpet sounding the recall or a signal for a new line of advance.

But the summary has to be accurate and impartial. With all a leader's other responsibilities, it requires a high level of natural ability and practice for them to be able to summarize succinctly at the right time, in such a way that the summary is instantly accepted as a true account of the proceedings to date.

Although *summarizing* is an especially important skill for a chairperson, all listeners can find it useful on occasions. A summary is a sign of listening, because it establishes whether or not you can select the salient points to the satisfaction of the speaker and the rest of the audience, if there is one.

A summary not only chops away much of the dead wood and foliage, it also provides a listening check, for other listeners will either accept your abbreviation or reject it. Thus a summary helps in the process of thought and digestion.

Idea 80: Always follow up with action points

Action this day.

Winston Churchill, British statesman
and former prime minister

Good follow-up is just as important as the meeting itself. Peter Drucker and I once discussed this point over a working lunch on strategic leadership. Peter instanced Alfred Sloan as a master of making sure things happened after meetings. Sloan, who headed General Motors from the 1920s until the 1950s, was, he told me, 'the most effective business executive I have known'.

Drucker had observed Sloan in action. He always announced the purpose at the beginning of a formal meeting. Then he listened. He rarely spoke himself except to clarify a misunderstanding and he never took notes. He summed up at the end, thanked the participants and left. Immediately afterwards he wrote a short memo to all those who had attended, summarizing the discussion and its conclusions, and listing the work assignments decided on in the meeting. He specified the executive who was to be accountable and the deadline for completion.

Clear, concise and definite minutes are certainly necessary. They should normally make clear who is to do what and by when, together with a deadline for reporting back progress.

> *'Any given meeting is either productive or a total waste of time. It usually depends on the leader.'*

Idea 81: Becoming an effective chairperson

Guests sleep well in the Inn of Decision.

Arab proverb

Good chairmanship is vital for effective meetings. The chair's task will sometimes pose problems, but a good chairperson can make sure that a meeting is punctual, covers the ground, keeps moving forward and makes the appropriate decisions. Beneath that process lies purposeful communication.

Your manner may do as much if not more than your words to encourage, or discourage, genuine communication. Humour, modesty and firmness have their own part to play.

As the leader's own task encompasses the creation of a warm, friendly but businesslike atmosphere, it is vital that you should check whether or not your manner aids and abets the promotion of good communication. In the right time and place, ask for feedback on this score.

If someone is asked to take action as a result of discussion of an item, the chairperson should check that the participant understands and accepts that action. Steps or actions thus agreed should normally carry a completion time.

Case study: The effective chairman

The Prime Minister shouldn't speak too much himself in Cabinet. He should start the show or ask somebody else to do so, and then intervene only to bring out the more modest chaps who, despite their seniority, might say nothing if not asked. And the Prime Minister must sum up . . . Particularly when a non-Cabinet minister is asked to attend, especially if it is his first time, the Prime Minister may have to be cruel. The visitor may want to show how good he is, and go on too long. A good thing is to take no chance and ask him to send the Cabinet a paper in advance . . . If somebody else looks like making a speech, it is sound to nip in with, 'Are you objecting? You're not? Right. Next business'. And the Cabinet can move on leaving in its wake a trail of clear, crisp uncompromising decisions. That is what government is about. And the challenge to democracy is to get it done quickly.

Clement Attlee, former UK Prime Minister

Eight Greatest Ideas for Successful Interviews

Idea 82: Four characteristics of interviews

There is more wisdom in listening than speaking.

Sudanese proverb

We can define an interview as a meeting, usually between two people, arranged with a clear purpose and with the roles of the participants well defined. The word itself comes from the French verb *s'entrevoir*, meaning 'to see each other'.

Interviews range from a meeting or conversation between a journalist or radio or television presenter and a person whose views are sought for publication or broadcasting, through oral examinations of candidates for a job or place in higher education, to an interrogation of a person by the police about a specific event, sometimes euphemistically known as 'helping the police with their inquiries'. What do interviews have in common?

1. They are usually prearranged, with the possible exception of a dismissal interview.
2. Both interviewer and, generally, interviewee need to prepare for them.
3. They all have a definite purpose, which should be clearly known to both participants.
4. They all centre on communication – 'the process by which meanings are exchanged between people through the use of a common set of symbols'.

Most managers think that they are good at conducting interviews, just as most of us think that we are good drivers. How would you assess your own ability in this respect? In fact interviewing, like driving, is an art with its advanced levels. But you don't have to be ill in order to get better. However proficient at interviewing you may believe yourself to be, there is always room for improvement.

Ask yourself
What are my strengths and weaknesses in one-to-one, work-related meetings?

Idea 83: Structuring the interview

Structuring or planning the interview is necessary if it is to avoid becoming a shapeless conversation. The amount of structure will depend on the purpose of the interview and your own experience. The more experienced you are, the less you will need a preplanned structure of questions to be asked. You should always, however, have a note of the main questions or issues you want to ask or raise.

Like games of chess, interviews have a beginning, middle and end. Each requires skill, as does making the transitions from one part to the other. This table may help to clarify this.

Opening	Introduce yourself and mention any other important factors.
	Confirm the purpose of the meeting straight away.
	Put the other person at ease.
	Try to encourage an atmosphere where both of you are relaxed, open-minded, committed to the purpose and prepared to discuss things calmly and frankly.
Middle	Keep your aim firmly in mind as you exchange information.
	Keep the discussion relevant, helpful and work oriented.
	Listen, or give the other person's replies or comments your thoughtful attention.
	Listen to the person as well as what they say, and so listen with your eyes as well as your ears.
	Make sure that you have covered the agenda.
Conclusion	Sum up the discussion.
	Describe the action you have decided or mutually agreed.
	Confirm the worthwhileness of the meeting.
	Avoid ending abruptly.
	Close on a positive note.

Idea 84: The skill of asking the right question

It is harder to ask a sensible question than to supply a sensible answer.

Persian proverb

Questions are the tools of interviewing or, more widely, of listening. The art of interviewing largely consists of asking the right questions at the right time. There are several different kinds of question, each with its pros and cons. It is useful to have them all in your repertoire, so that you don't get stuck like a broken record on only one type of question.

Question	Uses	Disadvantages
The yes/no question For example, 'Have you read this report?'	Good for checking facts. Establishes where a rough balance lies quickly (e.g. 'Are you healthy?').	Can force oversimplified answers (e.g. to the question 'Are you or are you not satisfied with your job?').
The closed question For example, 'How long have you worked here?'	Best where facts or data are sought. Form of question restricts answer to a limited area.	Can sound like an interrogation. Leaves little room for discussion or explanation.
The open-ended question For example, 'How do you see your career progressing?'	Good for opening up the exchange and discussion of information and ideas.	May invite long and rambling answers, leading to irrelevancies.

(Continued)

Question	Uses	Disadvantages
The leading question For example, 'Don't you agree that you should have done that weeks ago?'	Not very useful, unless you are trying to push someone in a certain direction.	The knowledge gained by a leading question is usually limited in value.
The loaded question For example, 'What do you think about the chief executive's stupid play for expansion in Europe?'	Limited, unless it's deliberately provocative.	A loaded question is charged with some hidden implication or underlying suggestion. It has a bias or prejudice built into it. It can also blow up in your face.
The prompt For example, 'So what did you do then?'	Keeps things moving, guiding the interviewee in content and direction. Clarifies if the other person has not understood what you want.	Can prematurely curtail or direct an interesting reply to an open-ended question.
The probe For example, 'What precisely was the extent of your budget responsibility in Canada?'	Obtains more information, following through from the general to the particular.	Can make it all sound like an interrogation.

Question	Uses	Disadvantages
The mirror For example, 'So you felt completely fed up at this point?'	A reflective way of checking whether or not you have received the other person's message accurately.	Be careful that you do not introduce a slight alteration of meaning: 'No I felt rather frustrated, but not fed up.'
The 'what-if?' question For example, 'Supposing we opened an office in the Gulf, would that interest you?	Making assumptions or creating situations imaginatively and asking what the interviewee would do.	Can force someone's hand or lad to unfulfilled expectations. Only yields hypothetical information.

Idea 85: Setting objectives

'Appraisal interview' is a familiar term in the lexicon of management. This is a regular interview, sometimes as infrequently as once or twice a year, when a manager sits down with their subordinate and appraises the work of the subordinate against their objectives. 'Don't tell me that the man is doing good work,' said Andrew Carnegie to one of his plant bosses. 'Tell me what good work he is doing.'

During an appraisal meeting you should create an environment where you can have a constructive dialogue with a subordinate (or superior or colleague, for that matter) on the following agenda:

- ◆ Past performance.
- ◆ Future work to be done, targets, priorities, standards and strategies.
- ◆ Matching perceptions of what each can reasonably expect from the other.
- ◆ Improving skills, knowledge and behaviour.

Remember that the performance appraisal interview has as its main purpose the improvement of an individual's work contribution. (It may have as its secondary purpose providing grounds for a salary review.)

There is a necessary condition that has to be met before you can hold an effective appraisal interview. If you haven't set or agreed objectives some months or weeks in advance, it is a waste of time to have an appraisal interview.

For while you can and should, of course, discuss interviewees' performance of the general or ongoing duties of their offices or jobs – what they are being paid for – it is much easier to do that if both of you know that some progressive objectives covering all or parts of the job will be under review.

Somehow people are less inclined to take on board suggestions or criticisms that come 'out of the blue' and relate to a general function of their job, such as being nice to customers.

Idea 86: Ten guidelines for appraising performance

The manager lives with the people he manages, he decides what their work is to be, he directs it, he trains them for it, he appraises it and, often, he decides their future. Being a manager is like being a parent, or a teacher. And in these relationships honourable dealings are not enough; personal integrity is of the essence.

Peter Drucker, *The Practice of Management* (1956)

1. *Ensure that the necessary data is available.*
    To substantiate discussion and keep it factual, all documents, reports, data or back-up information should be readily available for the interview.
2. *Put the other person at ease.*
    Both parties should try to be relaxed, open-minded, aware of the purpose of the meeting, committed to its purpose and prepared to discuss things calmly and frankly.
3. *Control the pace and direction of the interview.*
    Both parties have a part to play in controlling and influencing the pace and direction of the interview to keep it relevant, helpful and work oriented.
4. *Listen . . . listen . . . listen.*
    The most difficult part of the interview is for both parties to really listen to each other.
5. *Don't be destructively critical.*
    Where possible, people should be encouraged to be self-critical: critical of their own performance and motivated to improve. This approach goes a long way to removing unnecessary conflict from the meeting.

6. *Review performance systematically.*
    It is important to stick to the facts – facts that can be substantiated – and that's where the relevant back-up information comes in handy.

7. *Discuss future action.*
    This is an opportunity to discuss with one another, almost on equal terms, what has been done, how it can best be done, who will do it, when and to what standard.

8. *Be prepared to discuss potential or aspirations.*
    The question of the individual's potential for future promotion doesn't always arise, but it is wise to be prepared for it.

9. *Identify the essential training/development required.*
    The final part of the interview is usually devoted to discussing the training and counselling that may be required in order to carry out the agreed action plan.

10. *Avoid obvious pitfalls.*
    Such dangers as:
    - ◆ Talking too much and hogging the conversation.
    - ◆ Introducing unnecessary conflict.
    - ◆ Jumping to hasty conclusions.
    - ◆ Unjustly blaming others, particularly those who are not present to defend themselves.
    - ◆ Expecting the impossible, like wanting a person to change significant character traits overnight.
    - ◆ Making promises that neither party may be able to keep.

Idea 87: Constructive appraisal in action

Love, in the sense of seeking the good of the other person as well as the common good, stands here at the core of good communication.

Henry Ward Beecher,
American clergyman and abolitionist

Field Marshal Lord Montgomery was not only a great trainer of soldiers, he gave his generals some on-the-job training as well. In *A Full Life* (1956), General Sir Brian Horrocks recalled one such incident. It reveals Montgomery's ability to develop the individual, even at the higher levels of leadership.

Case study: Field Marshal Lord Montgomery

On the day after the battle [Alam Haifa] I was sitting in my headquarters purring with satisfaction. The battle had been won and I had not been mauled in the process. What could be better? Then in came a liaison officer from Eighth Army headquarters bringing me a letter in Monty's even hand. This is what he said:

> *Dear Horrocks,*
> *Well done – but you must remember that you are now a corps commander and not a divisional commander . . .*

He went on to list four or five things which I had done wrong, mainly because I had interfered too much with the tasks of my subordinate commanders. The purring stopped abruptly.

Perhaps I wasn't quite such a heaven-sent general after all. But the more I thought over the battle, the more I realized that Monty was right. So I rang him up and said, 'Thank you very much.'

I mention this because Montgomery was one of the few commanders who tried to train the people who worked under him. Who else, on the day after his first major victory, which had altered the whole complexion of the war in the Middle East, would have taken the trouble to write a letter like this in his own hand to one of his subordinate commanders?

Idea 88: How to give constructive criticism

He has a right to criticize who has a heart to help.

US President, Abraham Lincoln

The ability to accept, digest and act on constructive criticism is a sign of maturity. It is the insecure who ignore, deny or deflect accurate feedback when it is offered to them.

Here are some ground rules for giving constructive criticism.

Offer criticisms in private and do not spread them about

Nothing distresses people more than to be criticized in front of their colleagues or subordinates. Do it in private, and don't talk about your conversation to a third party.

Avoid long or predictable preambles

Avoid prefaces such as 'Listen. There's something I've wanted to tell you for a long time. It may hurt you, but . . . ' In these matters it is best to come to the point. Remember, too, that a smile in giving honest criticism can make the difference between resentment and reform.

Avoid preliminary positive evaluations that contain very little supplementary information, such as 'You are doing a fine job, but . . . ' Don't use insincere praise as a sweetener. 'He who praises everybody praises nobody,' wrote English author Samuel Johnson.

But of course, it is a key principle that constructive criticism will always be more readily received if you can preface it with some genuine and evidence-based praise.

Offer only constructive criticism of actions that can be changed

'No man, by taking thought, can add one cubit to his stature,' as the saying goes. It is useless to criticize people for characteristics that they cannot change.

Don't compare the person's behaviour with that of others

Comparisons predispose others not to listen, even when the criticism or complaint is justified.

Keep it as simple and as accurate as possible

Avoid overload. Try to make only one or two major criticisms at a time, rather than presenting a list of sixty or seventy! As the Chinese proverb says: 'Do not use a hatchet to remove a fly from your friend's forehead.'

Exaggerations intended for emphasis, signalled by such words as *always* and *never*, rob you of your accuracy and the psychological advantages that go with it. Moreover, instead of statements such as 'You are very idle', it may be more accurate to say 'You give me the impression of being lazy'. That 'impression' at least is an objective fact. And if more than one person has formed that impression it should have some weight.

Nor should the same point be endlessly repeated. The reward for good listening ought to be exemption from hearing the same short-coming discussed again.

Don't talk about other people's motives when making a complaint or criticism

Motives stand closer to the inner person than his or her actions, and to pass judgement on them can be interpreted as a censure of the whole person.

Always be able to back up your observations with some evidence or data. Thus an appraisal should never stray far from the facts. Avoid amateur psychology.

After making a criticism in good faith, don't apologize for it

An apology may fuel some inner doubt as to whether or not you had the right to say what you did. It is asking the other person to brace you against the stress of criticizing them. It imposes an unnecessary burden on them.

An apologetic tone and an embarrassed manner do neither of you any good. You do need moral courage, but by all means apologize if it transpires that you have got the facts wrong. It is more fitting to thank the person concerned for listening to your criticism or complaint.

> 'Tact is the art of making a point without making an enemy.'

Idea 89: How to take constructive criticism

Take each man's censure, but reserve your judgement.

William Shakespeare, *Hamlet*

You should work with your critic to identify the areas for improvement, like a fellow surgeon working around an operating table. What should matter to both of you is any improvement in your common work. Nor will you be distracted by imperfections in your appointed (or self-appointed) critic: truth is truth whether it comes from the mouths of angels or barmaids. Try to be grateful in advance for what you are about to receive. The following tips could help.

Be quiet while you are being criticized and make it clear that you are listening

Whether you agree or not is an issue to be discussed later.

Under no condition find fault with the person who has just criticized you

If they have used the wrong words or got a minor fact wrong, do not overreact, wait half an hour. If you counter-attack by reciprocating the criticism – 'Now I think about it, you come late to meetings too' – this implies that you interpret it as an insult. Or you become so busy in marshalling your own forces for the attack that you can neglect to heed what is actually being said.

Don't create the impression that the other person is destroying your spirit

Avoid any sign that your soul has been fractured by the criticism. It shows a lack of perspective on your part and it can appear as if you are trying to manipulate or put pressure on your interlocutor.

Don't try to change the subject

To do so is a blatant sign that you don't want to listen, that you are not open to constructive criticism. Besides, it is discourteous.

Don't caricature the complaint

If a person says you were *thoughtless*, don't ascribe to them the statement that you are irresponsible and then defend yourself against a charge that has not been made. The deliberate exaggeration of a charge against you is a tactic for avoiding it.

Convey to the other person that you understand their constructive criticisms

Paraphrasing or using a minor question is one good way of doing this. In effect you are saying that the message is received and noted.

To receive criticism well and to act on it is the ultimate badge of the good listener. If it is unjustified, as later certified by completely impartial 'appeal judges', the appraisal interview can still be creatively turned into an occasion for learning humility.

If you feel that the criticism is fully justified, or at least that there is something in it for further reflection, thank your critics for their time and effort. The have done you a personal favour; they have given you a present. 'Criticism is a study by which people grow more important and formidable at very small expense,' concluded the writer Samuel Johnson. Can you afford to ignore such valuable and free tuition?

> *When a man says you are a horse laugh at him. When two men assert that you are a horse, give it a thought. And when three men say you are a horse, you had better go and buy a saddle for yourself.*
>
> *Hungarian folk saying*

Ask yourself
When criticized, do I always try to grasp the point in its fullness before accepting or rejecting it?

Follow-up test

Giving presentations

☐ Have you identified the five key presentational skills that you need to master?

☐ Do you always profile the occasion: the subject, audience and location?

☐ Have you done your reconnaissance?

☐ Have you stated your objective or objectives at the beginning of your presentation and said why you think it or they are important?

☐ If you decide to use visual aids, do you ensure that they are well designed graphically and do you use them with skill?

☐ Do you have a reliable sense for knowing when one more rehearsal is really needed before an important presentation?

☐ Have you visualized yourself delivering the presentation: the opening, the middle section, the conclusion, questions/discussion and your final words of thanks?

☐ Do you have an effective routine – not involving alcohol! – for calming your nerves before you stand up and speak in public?

☐ Why do you think that speaking without notes enhances your effect as a public speaker?

Leading effective meetings

- ☐ Are your meetings well planned, informal, participative and guided by a common purpose?
- ☐ What three lessons about meetings have you learned from the best discussion leaders you have encountered?
- ☐ When did you last review your eight skills as a leader of discussion in meetings?
- ☐ 'The first rule for a leader is to take charge in a low-key way and to remain in charge.' Would you agree?
- ☐ Are you especially good at chairing all five types of managerial meetings?
- ☐ Do you make it a matter of pride to prepare for those meetings in which you will be involved, especially if you are going to chair them?
- ☐ Are you noted for your ability as a chairperson to summarize a discussion, both at intermediate points (where necessary) and also at the end?
- ☐ Is it clear after your meetings who is to do what and by when? Do you have an agreed way for monitoring progress?
- ☐ Have you asked for feedback on how you perform your role as chairperson of a meeting? If so, do you now have an accurate idea of your strengths and weaknesses?
- ☐ Do your meetings invariably start on time and end on time?

Successful interviews

☐ Do you use the simple framework of beginning, middle and end when you are structuring an interview in your mind?

☐ In your questioning technique can you use, if need be, any of the nine types of question?

☐ 'Appraising people without setting objectives with them some months prior is putting the cart before the horse.' Do you agree?

☐ How good are you at establishing rapport with a person you are about to interview?

☐ Do you have the moral courage to give constructive criticism to those who report to you? Do you have the skill and the tact needed to do it effectively?

☐ How would you judge whether or not a person has taken your advice?

☐ When receiving feedback from others, do you look for a pattern in their comments?

☐ Are you as good at giving justified praise and saying thank-you as you are at giving criticism and finding fault?

PART FIVE
Communicating in Organizations

The major mistake in communication is to believe that it happens of its own accord.

Anonymous

Organizations are essentially communication systems. In the old days organizations were staffed by two classes: the communicators (managers) and the communicated-to (the workers), with a third class, the 'white-collar workers' in the office, somewhere in between.

The immense impact of unprecedented change has completely altered that picture. Now everyone who works for an organization is responsible for good communication: *upwards*, *downwards* and *sideways*. Part Five profiles these essential directions or flows of information.

Completely integrated into this internal system are the two other key flows of information: *inwards* from the environment and *outwards* from organization to the environment. If these two major systems – 'inside the egg' and 'outside the egg' – are not even linked, let alone integrated in your organization, then I have some bad news for you and your colleagues: you are sailing on the *Titanic* and you should make your way to the lifeboats now.

Six Greatest Ideas for Organizational Communication

Idea 90: Organizations are communication systems

The first function of the executive is to develop and maintain a system of communication.

Chester Barnard, US business executive
and management expert

Large human organizations are rarely created at a stroke of the pen. They tend to evolve organically from working groups or teams, which in turn come about through the leadership of one or two people.

A team is an organization in microcosm. It is a whole made up of interdependent parts, each with its proper function, evolved to achieve a purpose that one person could not attain alone or unaided. The 'parts' in this case are other individuals. In an organization, the 'parts' are themselves teams or work groups.

Often organizers out to bring order to relative chaos do have some pre-determined scheme in mind, such as at the military system. But the military system merely reflects a more primitive or natural method of social ordering in large groups, which can be expressed as a simple model:

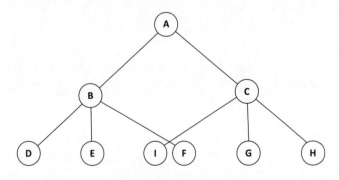

Elementary hierarchy

In a Bedouin tribe, for example, the sheikh pitches his tent in the middle and keeps an open door to all-comers. Members of the tribe are essentially free and equal, although in larger tribes there are subgroups of families or kin. Yet all have the right to take complaints or problems to the paramount sheikh for arbitration or solution.

Originally we were all tribal and the tribal tradition has been deeply influential. For example, being essentially egalitarian, tribal life was a direct ancestor of democracy. Why, then, did hierarchical organization emerge? One reason was the sheer size as tribes multiplied into nations that called for hierarchical organization. The other reason was military necessity. Armed tribal hordes turned into disciplined armies only so far as they were willing to accept the principle of hierarchy. The Roman army is still the copybook example or model of a very large organization.

In the elementary hierarchy diagram, A has overall leadership responsibility. The team leaders – D, E, F, G, H and I – report directly to B and C, who report in turn directly to A. All the elements of hierarchy are here. We have some rather cumbersome Latin-based words – subordinate, coordinate and superordinate – to describe where people come in the structure or order thus created:

◆ *Subordinates* – B and C are subordinate to A; all the others are subordinate to B and C as well; and the team members in each of the six groups are subordinate to their leaders, and all above.
◆ *Coordinates* – B and C are coordinates with each other, as are D, E, F, G, H and I. Team members are also coordinates within teams.
◆ *Superordinates* are all named leaders, A being the ultimate superordinate at the top of the pyramid.

Notice that hierarchy runs counter to tribal life, where people are on the same level as their leader and there are no interpositions of other levels. The tribal structure looks more like this:

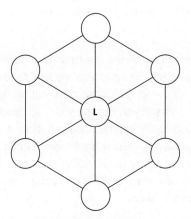

The tribal structure

The best way, in summary, is to look on your organization as essentially an orderly communication system, or set of systems, designed to get things done in the right way and at the right time. Always bear in mind the two-way directions or flows where the channels of communication need to carry clear and full water: downwards, upwards and sideways.

Idea 91: What needs to be communicated

We now know beyond a shadow of a doubt that there are three areas of need always present in all working groups and organizations:

1. To achieve the common task.
2. To be held together or to maintain themselves as cohesive unities.
3. The needs individuals bring with them into the group.

The main *content* of communication – information, ideas and knowledge, for example – in your organization should tie in with these three overlapping areas.

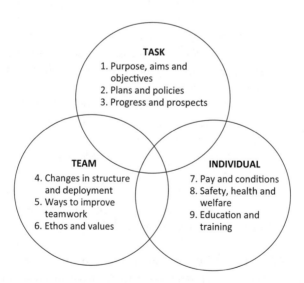

Communication Content In Three Circles

So what are you communicating?

- ◆ *Purpose, aim and objectives* – The core *purpose*, the key *aims* and the more tangible *objectives* of the organization are central in communication. Purpose answers the question 'Why?'
- ◆ *Plans and policies* – Planning answers the questions 'What', 'When?', 'How?', 'Where?' and 'Who?'. Planning may be at strategic, operational or team levels.
- ◆ *Progress and prospects* – Progress motivates; prospects motivate even more. This could include new products, innovations and positive changes in the pipelines.
- ◆ *Changes in structure and deployment* – Any organizational changes or alterations in the organization's deployment.
- ◆ *Ways to improve teamwork* – Anything that results in better team working, so that the various parts work in an integrated, harmonious whole.
- ◆ *Ethos and values* – The particular stars the organization steers by in the form of its corporate values; its spirit as opposed to its form.
- ◆ *Pay and conditions* – Anything that affects the remuneration, conditions of work or personal prospects for employment of individuals.
- ◆ *Safety, health and welfare* – Information that affects safety or security.
- ◆ *Education and training* – Whatever may contribute to the personal development, present competence and future capability of each individual member.

If you wish to be listened to, communicate to your hearers what is important, relevant or interesting. That principle applies as much to communicating in organizations as it does in personal life.

An individual without information cannot take responsibility. An individual with information cannot help but take responsibility.

Jan Carlson, former Chief Executive
of Scandinavian Airlines

Idea 92: Directions or flows of information

Communication is more than words. It is the imparting of meaning – voluntarily or involuntarily – and it flows. The most obvious direction of flow is *downwards* from the top to the bottom, or, if you prefer it, from the centre to the periphery.

Imagine a military command post where the general briefs his commanders, who in turn brief their captains. There are three levels of leadership at work here: strategic, operational and team.

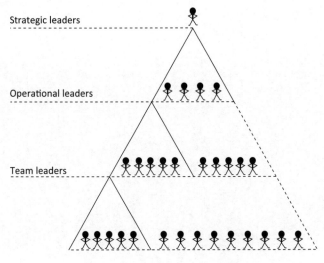

Three levels of leadership

You can see that there is a formal communication structure in place to transmit and translate the general's battle plan into action.

In the past, however, the three levels of leadership system has not been so good for *upwards* communication. What, you may ask, does a common soldier have to say to a general anyway? The answer was not much.

Better armies and navies did introduce constitutional systems for the upward transmission of grievances; never easy, because your immediate superior was often the source of your grievance and had no interest in passing your complaints upwards! In Nelson's enlightened navy, for example, every sailor had the right to approach an admiral directly and make a verbal or written complaint or grievance.

What has changed out of all recognition in modern organizations is the nature of operations. Now everyone has the responsibility of passing upwards any relevant information about, for instance, product performance or quality, customer needs or the responses of competitors.

The same competitive pressures have put a premium on teamwork. That in turn sorts out the organizations that have gone *sideways* from those that still have brick walls instead of chalk lines, dividing them like bulkheads into a series of watertight departments or businesses. Communication in successful organizations has become a three-way process: downwards, upwards and sideways.

This need for three-way communication results in some characteristic meetings that all good leaders establish in order to give communication a structure, such as:

- ◆ One-to-one meetings (weekly/fortnightly/monthly).
- ◆ Team meetings (weekly/fortnightly).
- ◆ Departmental meetings (monthly/quarterly).
- ◆ Awaydays (quarterly/biannual/annual).

Idea 93: The basic principle of organizational communication

Change throws up the need for leaders; leaders tend to create change. So never complain about change if you are a leader: it is what you are there for! It isn't all about change, however, for you have to balance change against the interests of continuity. That calls for judgement on the direction, scope and pace of change.

Leadership and communication cannot be separate either. Can you think of a good leader who is not a good communicator? Therefore it is leadership that stitches together the needs for effective change and good communication.

The first step is to see yourself in a role that requires *downwards*, *upwards* and *sideways* communication. Even as a strategic leader, you need to be able to communicate upwards to the board of directors or its equivalent. How should you do it?

The general principle of organizational communication is that the high-priority information should go by the best method of communication, which is face-to-face oral backed by writing.

There have been numerous attempts, some more successful than others, to systematize downwards, upwards and sideways communication by a series of regular meetings, such as briefing groups or liaison committees. Sometimes legislation in some countries has directed managers to introduce a particular system, such as works councils.

There is always a temptation to believe that when you have introduced a *system* – such as briefing groups or works councils – you have solved the communication problem.

But systems are subject to the law of atrophy: they tend to waste away. While systems can help, they are as good as the people operating them.

The winning combination is simple but durable systems peopled by committed and skilled communicators.

Idea 94: A listening leadership

If authority has no ears to listen, it has no head to govern.

Danish proverb

When managers do not listen they cease to be business leaders and revert to their former status as hired business administrators. So-called managers of this low calibre hardly listen at all: they *ignore, forget, distort* or *misunderstand* much of what they hear.

With a small group or team, as a leader you can communicate by informal personal contact. But organization implies that you communicate through formal channels, such as a military chain of command. A corollary is that if you work in organizations you have to respect these formal channels.

That doesn't mean to say that *informal* communication is totally absent from organizations; that is far from the case. There is plenty of information, discussion, conversation and networking in most organizations. But they should be essentially supplementary. If informal communication dominates it is probably because the formal communication system – the core of the organization – isn't working well.

In the context of an organization, *size* and *geographical spread* always put a strain on its power to communicate effectively. If *rapid change* is thrown into the equation the situation can be even worse. Conditions of change call for better communication, whereas size, geographical spread and elements of change itself are all working against you, like strong adverse currents.

To overcome potential problems you need a practical philosophy of communication that embraces the *content* of communication, the *directions* it must take and your *personal responsibility*. Prior to that, however, you need to be passionate about good communication.

Case Study: Portland Power Units

A large manufacturing company called Portland Power Units, makers of diesel engines, decide to invest in a large extension covering the adjacent car park.

Mark Evans, the new manager in charge, drew up an elaborate plan for the change so as to minimize any disruption of production while the walls were knocked down. He rearranged the schedules and ordered the new machinery from a firm that had supplied them last time.

The result was chaotic. The team leaders on the shop floor said that they had not been consulted and the building works would certainly hold up an important new order for China. The union said that the shift schedules were unworkable. 'They could also have saved a lot of money and technical problems if they ordered the new German machinery we saw when we toured that plant in Frankfurt,' added one of the team leaders.

Evans finally had to agree that he had not listened to those who knew most about the machinery, the layout of the new extension, the short schedules or the timetable for building works. His poor listening cost Portland Power Units just under £4 million. He is now working for another organization – possibly yours.

Ask yourself
Do I really *want* real two-way communication in this organization?

Idea 95: The art of inspiring while informing

One of the forgotten arts of communication is public speaking, in the sense of strategic or operational leaders standing up alone in front of their people and talking to them about the common task and *why* it is important. It is the art of inspiring while informing.

It is sometimes difficult to get people together in this way, especially if you are not the chief executive. But you should seize every opportunity of talking – and listening – to any significant groups of those who report indirectly to you.

One of the advantages of getting out of your office (if you still have one) and going around talking to people is that you can gauge the flow of communication as it courses through the arteries and veins of the network:

◆ Did that message you asked operational leaders to brief their team leaders with reach *this* team in another country?

◆ Why didn't this key suggestion for a new extension of service to existing major customers get communicated to the senior leadership team?

◆ How come our Holland branch cracked this particular production problem six months ago, but when I was in Spain last week they were still struggling with it?

◆ Why hasn't this young graduate manager in Scotland heard about our new leadership development strategy?

◆ Don't these rumours and false reports suggest that we are falling down in communication? Is it a systems problem or a people problem?

'Why is it that you spend so much time out of your office?' I once asked the president of Toyota. 'In the United Kingdom our top managers are often invisible, chained to their desks on the top floor of corporate headquarters.'

'There is a simple reason,' he replied. '*We do not make Toyota cars in my office.*'

Case study: Encouraging two-way communication

At times I received advice from friends, urging me to give up or curtail visits to troops. They correctly stated that, so far as the mass of men was concerned, I could never speak, personally, to more than a tiny percentage. They argued, therefore, that I was merely wearing myself out, without accomplishing anything significant, so far as the whole Army was concerned. With this I did not agree. In the first place I felt that through constant talking to enlisted men I gained accurate impressions of their state of mind. I talked to them about anything and everything: a favourite question of mine was to inquire whether the particular squad or platoon had figured out any new trick or gadget for use in infantry fighting. I would talk about anything so long as I could get the soldier to talk to me in return.

I knew, of course, that news of a visit with even a few men in a division would soon spread throughout the unit. This, I felt would encourage men to talk to their superiors, and this habit, I believe, promotes efficiency. There is, among the mass of individuals who carry the rifles in war, a great amount of ingenuity and initiative. If men can naturally and without restraint talk to their officers, the products of their resourcefulness becomes available to all. Moreover, out of the habit grows mutual confidence, a feeling of partnership that is the essence of esprit de corps. An army fearful of its officers is never as good as one that trusts and confides in its leaders.

General Dwight D. Eisenhower, former US President

Five Greatest Ideas for Delighting Your Customers

Idea 96: How to create a delighted customer

If you cannot smile do not open your shop today.

Chinese proverb

An organization needs good two-way communication with its hydra-headed environment: financial institutions, stakeholders, government, local society and the global community, to name but a few of its talking heads.

But the importance for every kind of organization of creating a delighted customer, the direct or indirect purchaser of its products or services, can hardly be overstated.

A huge range of factors can contribute to customer satisfaction, but your customers – both consumers and other businesses – are likely to take into account:

◆ How well your product or services matches customer needs.
◆ The value for money you offer.
◆ Your efficiency and reliability in fulfilling orders.
◆ The professionalism, friendliness and expertise of your employees.
◆ How well you keep your customers informed.
◆ The after-sales service you provide.

Notice how good communication is essential at every point in your business's relationship with its customers.

Do you know the remark that appears most often in customer complaint emails throughout the world? *Will you people ever listen?* So, above all, listen to what customers have to say.

To communicate really well with your customers, you and your organ-ization must handle complaints as personally as possible, by a meeting or phone call in preference to a letter or email.

Always communicate any product or service and pricing changes to customers well in advance. People don't like unpleasant surprises, but giving both advance notice and the reasons takes away some of the sting.

Remember that customers (and suppliers) communicate with others about you. Make sure that what they say is good news.

'Good things sell themselves; bad things have to be advertised.'

Idea 97: The art of building up goodwill

Common sense is not always common practice.

Modern proverb

Some people see their customers as things, economic pawns or statistics on a graph, rather than as people. Wiser business leaders think differently. They understand that the relationship between them and their customers is the cornerstone of sustained business success.

The very word *customer* implies an incipient relationship. Derived from the word *custom*, a habitual use or practice, a customer is a person who buys products or services from a shop or business, usually systematically or frequently. If they buy from you just once they are purchasers, not customers.

It is in your interest to build on that embryonic relationship. Turn it into one of positive goodwill and mutual loyalty, based on an established reputation both for quality and for service. Why? Let me hand you over to one who can answer your question with far more authority than I can: John Spedan Lewis.

He founded the British department store and supermarket chain known today as the John Lewis Partnership, a group renowned for its customer service. Writing in 1917, he said:

> *If we rely upon our value alone we shall obtain considerable success. If to our value we add constant and careful cultivation of all the other arts of building up and maintaining good will, we shall be vastly more formidable to our competitors and do a good deal better.*

One of those arts or skills lies in obtaining, interpreting and acting on feedback from your customer base. For example, National Express, one of the UK's leading travel companies, invites passengers to send text messages to the organization while riding on its coaches. No one has a better idea of customer needs than your customers. Make sure that you are listening to them.

Ask yourself

Can I list four ways of enabling customers in my field of business to give us feedback?

Think of these ways as nets that will enable you to harvest their ideas and suggestions for improvements in both your products or services and also, equally importantly, your after-sales service.

'Quality in a product or service is not what you put into it but what the customer gets out of it.'

Idea 98: How to respond to customer complaints

Your most unhappy customers are your greatest sources of learning.

Bill Gates, founder of Microsoft

You are bound to face situations when things go wrong from a customer's point of view. Don't be dismissive of your customer's problem, even if you are convinced you're not at fault. Often you will be dealing with a customer's perceptions, and in this context they are as important as the facts of the case.

Although it sounds like a paradox, a customer with a complaint represents a genuine opportunity for your business:

◆ If you handle the complaint successfully, your customer is likely to prove to be more loyal in the future as if nothing had gone wrong in the present.

◆ People willing to complain are rare. Your complaining customer may be alerting you to a problem that has been experienced by many others who silently took their custom elsewhere. Remember to thank them for doing you this favour.

Complaints should be dealt with courteously, sympathetically and above all swiftly. Sympathy or empathy is important because it shows that you understand and take into account the customer's disturbed feelings. Strike a positive note from the beginning.

Make sure that your business has an established procedure for dealing with customer complaints and that it is known to all your employees. At the very least it should involve:

- ◆ Listening sympathetically to establish the details of the complaint.
- ◆ Recording the details together with relevant material, such as a sales receipt or damaged goods.
- ◆ Offering rectification, whether by repair, replacement or refund.
- ◆ Appropriate follow-up action, such as a letter of apology or a phone call to make sure that the problem has been made good.

If you're proud of the way you solve problems and rectify errors – by offering no-questions refunds, for example – make sure that your customers know about it. Your excellence at dealing with customer problems is one more way to stay ahead of your competitors.

Always remember, however, that it is still more excellent not to create the problems or commit the mistakes in the first place. And you will find, too, that it is far more cost-effective!

> *'The quality of your service depends on the quality of your people.'*

Idea 99: Don't make promises unless you keep them

Well done is better than well said.

Benjamin Franklin, one of the
Founding Fathers of America

All human relationships, professional and personal, depend on trust. And it is truth that creates trust. Conversely, untruth in all its guises – dishonesty, lying, insincerity, deviousness, lack of integrity – erodes and eventually destroys trust between people.

A promise is a verbal or written engagement to do (or not to do) some specific act. If you don't do as you promise, then in the eyes of the other person you have placed yourself firmly and squarely in the untruth camp. How does that feel?

There is then a domino effect. Trust levels fall, and that in turn reduces the existing goodwill. As the relationship deteriorates, communication also breaks down. In frustration, the customer eventually takes their custom elsewhere. Dead promises, dead business.

Therefore don't make promises unless you will keep them. Not *intend* to keep them, *will* keep them. If you say 'Your new bedroom furniture will be delivered on Tuesday', make sure that it is. Otherwise, don't say it.

The same principle applies across the board, to deadlines or client appointments, for example. It also applies, of course, to your own internal market at work: never say to a colleague that you will do something and then don't do it.

If you are 'seriously let or hindered' from keeping your promise, then communicate that fact to the customer without delay, together with reasons – not excuses.

Ask yourself
Can I think of an example in the last six months when someone selling me a product or service did not honour the promise they made to me? And when I remonstrated, they made more promises, which they did not keep either?

◆ How did I feel?
◆ Would I do business with that company again?
◆ Have I recommended them to my friends?

'You will be judged by what you do, not what you say.'

Idea 100: The delighted customer

It is self-evident that your business needs customers if it is to survive. But if you wish to enjoy sustained business success, you need to create *satisfied* customers. That is a feeling the customer has that your product or service has met their expectations.

Now let's take it a step further. Why not created *delighted* customers? The delighted customer has a feeling much stronger than satisfaction, or the 'feel good' factor. It is the feeling that the products or services in question, including the quality of the relationship, have exceeded their expectations, often by a great margin.

How do you achieve that result? By going the extra mile. That means to make an extra effort, to do more than is strictly asked or required. It looks a bit foolish; you won't find traffic jams on the extra mile. But there is wisdom in the generosity of spirit that the world calls folly.

The law of reciprocity (Idea 5) teaches us that if we give more generously, we will tend to receive more generously; eventually, that is, and maybe a different kind. But any thought of how you will profit from the customer by going the extra mile should be far from your mind. Do it because it is the right thing to do.

There is, however, one almost inevitable reward of creating the delighted customer that I should like to remind you about.

Customers have long memories. In their conversations for months to come, the delighted customer will be spreading the word about your products and services, building your reputation for you. You will never find a better salesperson than word of mouth – and you don't even have to pay her wages!

Whether it's a coupon for a future discount, additional information on how to use the product or a genuine smile, people love to get more than they were expecting. And don't think that a gesture has to be large to be effective. The local art framer that I sometimes use attaches a package of picture hangers to every picture he frames. A small thing, but his customers certainly notice and appreciate it. It is your generosity of spirit that counts, not the size of the gift.

> *'Always give people more than they expect to receive.'*

Follow-up test

Communicating in organizations

☐ Do you give priority to establishing and maintaining in proper working order good systems of communication – downwards, upwards and sideways – in your organization?

☐ Have you a clear idea of what *must*, what *should* and what *might* be communicated in this three-way system?

☐ Do you ensure that *must-know* information goes by the best method of communication: face to face and backed up in writing?

☐ Are you a listening leader yourself?

Delighting the customer

☐ Do you know the product or service you are offering the customer back to front? In other words, are you an expert in your field?

☐ What parts of your organization's vision or mission statement and supporting set of values relate specifically to the customer?

☐ 'We say that we are customer-centric but we aren't really – it is all lip-service.' Does that comment apply to your company: Wholly? Partially? Not at all?

☐ How well do you keep customers informed of any changes in the pipeline?

- ☐ Does your organization have a reputation for really listening to its customers?
- ☐ Do you regard complaining customers as opportunities to create new friends and to improve your business?
- ☐ Are you free – no, I mean really free – of the pernicious habit of making promises to customers that you have not the slightest intention of keeping, just to buy a little time?
- ☐ Are you always looking for ways, however small or incremental, to transform a satisfied customer into a delighted one?

About John Adair

John Adair is the business guru who invented Action Centred Leadership (ACL) in the 1970s, now one of the best-known leadership models in the world. Organizations worldwide use it to develop their leadership capability and management skills. ACL is being successfully applied in engineering companies, retailers, local authorities, financial institutions and universities. The British armed services base their leadership training on it.

John's company, Adair International, provides ACL development programmes, Accredited Trainer programmes and consultancy around the world, via regional partnerships with training providers in the UK, Australia, New Zealand, the Middle East and India.

John is the author of more than 40 books, translated into many languages, and numerous articles on history, leadership and management development.

Index